slow cooking
through the
seasons

carolyn humphries

foulsham

The Publishing House, Bennetts Close, Cippenham, Slough,
Berkshire, SL1 5AP, England

Foulsham books can be found in all good bookshops and direct from
www.foulsham.com

ISBN: 978-0-572-03421-4

Copyright © 2008 W. Foulsham & Co. Ltd

Cover photograph © James Murphy

A CIP record for this book is available from the British Library

The moral right of the author has been asserted

Other books for your slow cooker:
Slow Cooking from Around the World (978-0-572-03289-0)
New Recipes for Your Slo-cooker (978-0-572-02636-3)
Real Food from Your Slo-cooker (978-0-572-02536-6)
Slow Cooking for Yourself (978-0-572-03150-3)
Slow Cooking from Around the Mediterranean (978-0-572-03323-1)
Slow Cooking Curry and Spice Dishes (978-0-572-03406-1)

Printed in Great Britain by Mackays Ltd, Chatham, Kent

CONTENTS

INTRODUCTION

When I was a child, we had tangerines only at Christmas time, apples and pears in the autumn and through the winter, and parsnips weren't considered any good until the frost had got to them. Winter food meant stews with lots of root vegetables, because that's what was around, and we looked forward to the sweet rosy decadence of strawberries in June (usually with clotted cream from the farm by the river, just out of town). Chickens were a luxury and we went mushroom picking early on October mornings, when the dew was on the grass.

Now thanks to – or rather because of – international transport, refrigeration and freezing, you can get just about any food, any time of the year from all over the world. But is that an improvement? Emphatically, no!

I don't argue that it's great to be able to enjoy exotic foods that we don't grow here but even they have proper seasons when they are ripe and ready for eating, rather than being plucked from their source in their infancy to mature artificially en route. I'm sure you've had nectarines that just don't ripen but go wrinkled and taste like cardboard, or Californian plums like mini cannon balls and as sour as vinegar. So it's worth knowing when foreign foods are at their best too. We don't want to turn the clock back to when we could eat only what was grown locally but we should celebrate what is in season and buy it whenever we can. Whether that be enjoying the abundance of fish that is caught off our shores, eating the fruit and vegetables that are produced in the vicinity or meat that is reared on our own farms, we can and should enjoy our own food. It is vital for the environment and our economy, and simply because it tastes better! Why buy apples from South Africa when ours are in season or broccoli from Spain when we have acres of it here at the same time? It doesn't make sound food or environmental sense.

I'm not saying you should never buy foreign apples again, but do buy home-grown when they are available. If they're not, consider ethical trading when you shop. The Fairtrade Foundation is an independent body offering disadvantaged producers in the developing world a better deal for their produce. Many of the goods sold through the Foundation, such as bananas, citrus, mangoes, pineapples, avocados, coffee, tea, cocoa, dried fruit, sugar, spices, rice and fruit juices, are not even produced here, so they make excellent additions to home-bought produce. By actively seeking them out (even if it means paying a few pence more), you are making a much-needed difference to people who really need your help. The more we buy, the more products will become available and the cheaper they will become. That's simple economics.

So why seasonal slow cooking? Well, for a start, using a slow cooker is a fuel-saving way of cooking – it uses only about as much electricity as a light bulb, which is far less than using your conventional cooker – another plus for your carbon footprint. It's also a great way to enjoy all those locally grown vegetables and home-farmed meats, to make the most of the gluts of summer and autumn fruits and even to celebrate the pick of the catch as slow cooking keeps everything succulent, full of flavour and a sheer pleasure to eat.

For each month you'll find information on what's available, with home-grown food at the peak of its season in italics. Not all of it is suitable for slow-cooking but I've included a full list to help you learn – or perhaps re-learn – when foods are in season. You may be surprised by how many of them work well in the slow cooker. There's a whole host of deliciously different recipe ideas for heart-warming soups and rich, evocative casseroles, which you might expect, but perhaps you won't have imagined the range of wonderful custards, pies and desserts, whole seafood and even a meaty terrine to get your teeth into.

USING YOUR SLOW COOKER

1 Stand the electric base on a level, heat-resistant surface. Do not use on the floor.

2 Do not preheat your pot unless your manufacturer's instructions tell you to.

3 Put the ingredients in the ceramic crock pot, then put the pot in the base.

4 Add boiling liquid.

5 Cover with the lid and select the cooking temperature – High, Medium (if you have it) or Low. Note that some smaller cookers cook quite quickly on High, so you may find that cooking on the Low setting is preferable, particularly if you are not going to be there to keep an eye on things or are cooking only a smallish quantity.

6 Cook for the recommended time. If there is a range of time, check after the shorter time given; this will usually be sufficient for most cookers but the food won't spoil if it is cooked for the extra time.

7 Taste, stir and re-season, if necessary.

8 Switch off the cooker and remove the crock pot using oven gloves.

COOKING TIPS FOR THE SLOW COOKER

- Any of your usual soup, stew or casserole recipes can be cooked in your slow cooker but liquid doesn't evaporate as much as it does when cooking conventionally, so cut down the liquid content by 30–50 per cent (not necessary for soups) or increase the flour or cornflour (cornstarch) thickener by a third. You can always add a little extra liquid at the end of cooking, if necessary.
- Use a crock pot suitable for the quantity of food you want to cook. It should be at least ⅓–½ full for the best results (but for foods like ribs or chicken wings, a single layer is fine if you have a large pot). Don't use a small pot and pack the food in tightly to the top or the heat won't be able to penetrate the food – just as when cooking conventionally. But, conversely, don't have too little either. For instance, one chop in the pot will overcook unless the pot is filled up to at least a third with liquid. So, if cooking for one, you may need to double the amount of liquid to be on the safe side.
- If preparing food the night before you wish to start cooking, store the ingredients in the fridge overnight. Put them in the crock pot in the morning and cover with boiling liquid or sauce before cooking.
- Dried beans must be boiled rapidly in water for at least 10 minutes before adding to your crock pot, to destroy toxins in them.
- If you want a brown finish to meat or poultry, fry it quickly in a frying pan before adding it to the crock pot.
- For many dishes, it is best to quickly fry onions before adding them – the flavour is completely different from when they are slow cooked from raw.
- Make sure all frozen foods are thawed before use.
- Cut root vegetables into small, even-sized pieces and put them towards the bottom of the pot as they will take longer than the meat to cook.

- Do not cook too large a joint or bird in the crock pot (though you can get quite a large one in – see my festive bird recipe on page 120). It should fit in the pot with at least a 2.5 cm/1 in headspace. If unsure, cut the joint or bird in half before cooking (it will then cook quicker, as when cooking conventionally).
- When cooking soups, make sure there is a 5 cm/2 in headspace in the pot to allow for bubbling during cooking.
- Most foods can be slow cooked but pasta (unless pre-cooked) and seafood should be added for the last hour, and cream at the end of cooking. All the recipes in this book tell you how and when to do this.
- Most foods can be cooked on High or Low (or Medium or Auto-cook if you have these settings). Fish, rice and egg-based dishes, however, are best cooked on Low. Fish will cook in 1–2 hours maximum.
- If you are planning on being out all day, opt for cooking on Low, then there is little or no chance of the meal ruining even if you are late (particularly if you don't have a programmable slow cooker).
- Do not open the lid unnecessarily during cooking as heat will be lost. If you remove it to add extra ingredients or to stir more than once or twice, you may need to add an extra 10 minutes at the end (but in most cases there is sufficient cooking time built in to allow for this).
- Should there be too much liquid at the end of cooking, strain it into a saucepan and boil rapidly for several minutes until reduced to the quantity you require, or thicken it with a little flour or cornflour (cornstarch) blended with a little water.
- When the food is cooked, the cooker can be switched off and left for up to 30 minutes. The food will still be piping hot. If you need to leave food keeping hot for longer, switch to Low (this isn't suitable for egg-based, rice or pasta dishes).
- If you are unsure whether a joint of meat or a bird is cooked through, insert a meat thermometer at the end of cooking.
- You can use the crock pot to keep hot drinks, such as mulled wine, warm or for hot dips or fondues. Keep the pot on the Low setting.

LOOKING AFTER YOUR SLOW COOKER

- Do not put the crock pot or the lid in the oven, freezer or microwave, on the hob or under the grill (broiler).
- Do not plunge the hot pot into cold water after cooking, as this may cause it to crack.
- Do not leave the whole pot soaking in water as the base is unglazed and porous so will absorb the water. You may, however, leave water in the pot to soak it before washing.
- Do not preheat the cooker before adding the ingredients (unless your manufacturer's instructions tell you to).
- Do not use the slow cooker to reheat food.
- Do not leave uncooked food in the slow cooker when it is not switched on (so never put it in there overnight ready to switch on in the morning. Store the ingredients in the fridge).
- Do not use abrasive cleaners on the crock pot – but it will be dishwasher safe.
- Do not immerse the electric base in water; simply unplug it and wipe it clean with a damp cloth.

COOKING TIMES

Some crock pots now have three cooking settings but others have only two. I have cooked most foods on High or Low as they will be relevant to all. Use Medium for any of them, if you have it, and adjust the times according to the chart below.

Some cookers also have Auto-cook. Follow your manufacturer's guidelines to use it. I recommend you use Low if you are going to be out all day.

This chart also shows you the approximate conversion times from conventionally cooked soups, stews and casseroles, should you want to try your own recipes (but remember to reduce the liquid by at least a third). Always check your manufacturer's instructions too as their times may vary slightly.

The more you use your slow cooker, the more you will become used to the correct times for your own model.

Conventional cooking time	Slow cooking time in hours		
	High	**Medium**	**Low**
15–30 minutes	1–2	2–3	4–6
30 minutes–1 hour	2–3	3–4	5–7
1–2 hours	3–4	4–6	6–8
2–4 hours	5–6	6–8	8–12

NOTES ON THE RECIPES

- Most of these recipes are best cooked in a large oval 6.5 litre slow cooker but the majority can be cooked in a smaller round 3.5 litre cooker. Remember that some small models cook quite quickly on High, so you may prefer the Low setting.
- All ingredients are given in imperial, metric and American measures. Follow one set only in a recipe. American terms are given in brackets.
- The ingredients are listed in the order in which they are used in the recipe.
- All spoon measures are level: 1 tsp=5 ml; 1 tbsp=15 ml.
- Eggs are medium unless otherwise stated.
- Where possible, choose organic, free-range, outdoor-reared produce and certainly avoid intensively reared meat and poultry. If buying foreign charcuterie etc. (because I'm not suggesting you should never have imported foods ever again!), make sure it is labelled, at least, 'farm assured', which offers some guarantees of acceptable animal welfare.
- Always wash, peel, core and seed, if necessary, fresh produce before use.
- Seasoning is very much a matter of personal taste. Taste the food before serving and adjust to suite your own palate.
- Fresh herbs are great for garnishing and adding flavour. Pots of them are available in all good supermarkets. Keep your favourite ones on the windowsill and water regularly. Jars of ready-prepared herbs, such as coriander (cilantro), and frozen ones – chopped parsley in particular – are also very useful. Don't use dried for garnishing.
- When I call for stock, use fresh if possible, or make up the equivalent with stock concentrate, cubes or powder.
- All can and packet sizes are approximate as they vary from brand to brand.

JANUARY

Roots and tubers are in abundance – perfect fodder for slow cooking. Enjoy them in soups, stews and casseroles and experiment with the different varieties available to vary colour, flavour and texture. Game birds are still in season and there is plenty of great fish around. Citrus fruits from overseas are at their peak – you'll notice the difference in the flavour and fragrance of the soft citrus (such as clemetines and satsumas) available now from that of the same fruits in the shops a few months ago.

Vegetables
Beetroot (red beets)
Brussels sprouts
Brussels tops
Cabbages (green, red, white)
Carrots
Celeriac (celery root)
Celery
Chicory (Belgian endive)
Curly endive (frisée lettuce)
Curly kale
Jerusalem artichokes
Leeks
Lettuces
Onions
Pak choi
Parsnips
Potatoes (old, maincrop)
Rhubarb (forced)
Salsify and scorzonera
Shallots
Spring (collard) greens
Swedes (rutabaga)
Sweet potatoes
Swiss chard
Turnips

Fruit and nuts
Apples (Cox's, Bramleys)
Avocados (Fuerte)
Black grapes
Clementines
Grapefruit
Lemons
Mangoes
Oranges
Passion fruit
Pears (Conference, Comice)
Pineapples
Pomegranates
Satsumas
Seville oranges
Tangerines
Walnuts

Meat, poultry and game
Duck
Goose
Guinea fowl
Hare
Partridge
Pheasant (England, not Scotland)
Snipe

Venison
Wild duck (mallard)
Woodcock
Wood pigeon

Fish and seafood
Brill
Clams
Cockles
Cod
Crabs
Haddock
Hake
Halibut
John Dory
Lemon sole
Monkfish
Mussels
Oysters
Plaice
Turbot
Whiting

Produce in *italics* is UK seasonal fare at its peak.

This is a lovely, cheering soup with rich, earthy flavours, and the chilli, cumin and ginger bring a wonderful spicy warmth. Try substituting knobbly Jerusalem artichokes for the sweet potato; don't bother to peel them, just scrub them to remove the dirt and chop them up. If you don't like coriander, use fresh parsley for the garnish or add a few finely chopped roasted peanuts.

spicy sweet potato and peanut potage

SERVES 4

15 ml/1 tbsp groundnut (peanut) oil
1 leek, chopped
30 ml/2 tbsp tomato purée (paste)
75 ml/5 tbsp smooth peanut butter
1.5 ml/¼ tsp chilli powder
2.5 ml/½ tsp ground cumin
5 ml/1 tsp grated fresh root ginger
1.2 litres/2 pts/5 cups chicken or
  vegetable stock

1 fairly large sweet potato, peeled
  and cut into small dice
1 large potato, peeled and cut into
  small dice
Salt and freshly ground black pepper
15 ml/1 tbsp chopped fresh
  coriander (cilantro)

1 Heat the oil in a frying pan. Add the leek and fry gently for 2 minutes, stirring.

2 Blend in the tomato purée, peanut butter, spices and stock. Bring to the boil, stirring.

3 Put the sweet potato and ordinary potato in the crock pot. Pour the peanut mixture over and season lightly. Cover and cook on High for 3 hours or Low for 6 hours until all the vegetables are tender.

4 Stir, taste and re-season, if necessary. Serve sprinkled with the coriander.

Using the slow cooker is a great way to cook dried beans as they can be left without the possibility of boiling dry. However, if you prefer, you can use a drained 410 g/14½ oz/large can of beans and start the recipe at step 2. This hearty soup is a great way to celebrate the best of the winter crops – and it will also prove very economical at this time of year.

country vegetable soup
with white beans

SERVES 4

100 g/4 oz/⅔ cup dried haricot (navy) beans, soaked in cold water for several hours or overnight
30 ml/2 tbsp olive oil
1 onion, finely chopped
1 leek, thinly sliced
1 celery stick, finely chopped
1 carrot, finely diced
½ small swede (rutabaga), finely diced

1 large turnip, finely diced
400 g/14 oz/1 large can of chopped tomatoes
15 ml/1 tbsp tomato purée (paste)
2.5 ml/½ tsp dried oregano
A good pinch of unrefined caster (superfine) sugar
Salt and freshly ground black pepper
1 vegetable stock cube
Finely grated Parmesan cheese for sprinkling

1   Drain the beans and place in a saucepan. Just cover with cold water, bring to the boil and boil rapidly for 10 minutes to remove any toxins. Tip into the crock pot, cover and cook on High for 2–3 hours or Low for 4–6 hours until tender.

2   Heat the oil in a large saucepan. Add the onion and leek and fry, stirring, for 2 minutes. Add to the beans with all the remaining vegetables.

3   Add the can of tomatoes, 2 canfuls of water, the tomato purée, oregano, sugar and some salt and pepper to the saucepan. Crumble in the stock cube. Bring to the boil, stirring, then pour into the crock pot, cover and cook on High for 3 hours or Low for 6 hours.

4   Taste and re-season, if necessary. Ladle into warm bowls and serve sprinkled with grated Parmesan cheese.

This fish recipe makes a lovely change from the usual meat-based lasagne. It's a quickly prepared dish with loads of flavour and lots of texture, but as it takes just 2 hours to cook, it's not one to leave all day. You can, however, allow it to cook for a further hour, if absolutely necessary; or it will still keep hot without spoiling for 30 minutes after the cooker has been turned off.

whiting fillet lasagne with celery

SERVES 4

Sunflower or grapeseed oil for greasing
295 g/10½ oz/1 medium can of condensed celery soup
6 rectangular no-need-to-precook green lasagne sheets
550 g/1¼ lb whiting fillets, skinned
30 ml/2 tbsp tomato purée (paste)
Salt and freshly ground black pepper
400 g/14 oz/1 large can of chopped tomatoes
1 garlic clove, crushed

30 ml/2 tbsp sliced stoned (pitted) black olives
2.5 ml/½ tsp dried basil
A good pinch of unrefined caster (superfine) sugar
50 g/2 oz/½ cup grated Cheddar cheese
30 ml/2 tbsp chopped fresh parsley to garnish

TO SERVE:
A curly endive (frisée) salad

1 Lightly oil a shallow rectangular dish that will fit inside a large crock pot. Put a spoonful of the soup in the dish and spread it out.

2 Lay two lasagne sheets, side by side in the dish, breaking them to fit, if necessary.

3 Top with half the whiting fillets, laid side by side and head to tail. Smear with half the tomato purée and season lightly.

4 Mix together the tomatoes, garlic, olives, basil and sugar. Season to taste, then spoon half over the fish. Top with two more lasagne sheets, then repeat the fish and tomato layers.

5 Top with the remaining lasagne, then spoon the remaining soup over and sprinkle with the cheese. Place the dish in the crock pot and pour 1 cm/½ in of boiling water around. Cover and cook on Low for 2 hours until the pasta and fish feel tender when a knife is inserted down through the centre.

6 Sprinkle with the parsley and serve with a curly endive salad.

Hearty and warming, this casserole is the ideal dish to welcome you home after work on a cold winter's day. Parsnips have always been happy bedfellows with beef and here they add rich earthy sweetness; but to ring the changes you could use 3 large carrots or a medium-sized swede instead. The sesame seeds add a nutty flavour and texture.

braised steak with parsnips and sesame-coated potatoes

SERVES 4

45 ml/3 tbsp sunflower oil
2 large onions, halved and sliced
2 large parsnips, diced
60 ml/4 tbsp plain (all-purpose) flour
2 bay leaves
700 g/1½ lb lean braising steak, trimmed and cut into large chunks
300 ml/½ pt/1¼ cups boiling beef stock

4 large potatoes, scrubbed and quartered
30 ml/2 tbsp sesame seeds
Salt and freshly ground black pepper
30 ml/2 tbsp chopped fresh parsley

TO SERVE:
Lightly steamed green cabbage

1   Heat 15 ml/1 tbsp of the oil in a large frying pan, add the onions and fry, stirring, for 3 minutes until lightly golden. Transfer to the crock pot. Add the parsnips to the onions, sprinkle the flour over and toss well. Tuck in the bay leaves.

2   Heat the remaining oil in the frying pan, add the meat and brown quickly on all sides. Transfer to the crock pot with a draining spoon. Pour the boiling stock over the beef and stir thoroughly.

3   Toss the potatoes in the frying pan to coat in any remaining oil and the pan juices. Add the sesame seeds and toss well. Arrange the potatoes around the edge of the pot, spooning any seeds left in the pan over the potatoes. Season everything well, then cover and cook on High for 4 hours or Low for 8 hours or until meltingly tender.

4   Discard the bay leaves, taste and re-season, if necessary. Transfer the beef, potatoes and parsnips in their sauce to warm plates and sprinkle with the parsley. Serve with lightly steamed cabbage.

Duck really lends itself to Asian-style cooking. The saltiness of soy sauce, the sweetness of pomegranate and pepper and the fragrance of ginger and garlic mingled with the crunchiness of lightly cooked pak choi make this a delightful dish in a slow cooker. Do use pomegranate molasses if you can – but you can substitute grenadine syrup if necessary.

duck with pomegranate and pak choi

SERVES 4

60 ml/4 tbsp soy sauce, plus extra for sprinkling
30 ml/2 tbsp boiling water
15 ml/1 tbsp pomegranate molasses
30 ml/2 tbsp unrefined light brown sugar
10 ml/2 tsp grated fresh root ginger
1 large garlic clove, crushed

1 oven-ready duck, cut into quarters, or 4 duck portions
1 red (bell) pepper, cut into very thin strips
4 slabs of dried Chinese egg noodles, or 300 g/11 oz fresh
4 heads of pak choi, shredded
Seeds from 1 pomegranate

1 Mix together the soy sauce, water, pomegranate molasses, sugar, ginger and garlic in the crock pot. Add the duck and the pepper strips and turn to coat completely in the marinade. Cover and cook on Low for 5–6 hours until tender.

2 Just before the end of the cooking time, cook the noodles, if using dried, according to the packet directions and drain.

3 When the duck is cooked, carefully lift the portions out of the pot and keep warm. Spoon off all the excess fat and add the pak choi and noodles to the pot. Toss well and leave for 2 minutes until piping hot. Spoon into large bowls and top with the duck. Sprinkle with the pomegranate seeds and serve with extra soy sauce sprinkled over.

This is a lovely rich, creamy dish, with a cheese and breadcrumb topping to give texture. The long slow cooking really enhances the flavour of the leeks and potatoes. Parboiling the potatoes helps to ensure even cooking and stops them discolouring during cooking. Garlic lovers can add one or two crushed garlic cloves in between the layers.

gratin of leeks
and potatoes

SERVES 4

25 g/1 oz/2 tbsp butter
2 large potatoes, sliced
2 leeks, trimmed and sliced
Salt and freshly ground black pepper
300 ml/½ pt/1¼ cups single (light)
   cream

40 g/1½ oz/¾ cup fresh
   breadcrumbs
50 g/2 oz/½ cup grated Gruyère
   (Swiss) cheese

1 Grease a shallow heatproof dish that will fit in a large oval crock pot with a little of the butter.

2 Parboil the potato slices in water for 2 minutes, then drain well. Layer the potato and leek slices in the dish, seasoning between each layer.

3 Pour the cream over and cover the dish with foil. Place in the crock pot and pour in enough boiling water around to come half-way up the sides of the dish. Cover and cook on Low for 5–6 hours until really tender.

4 Melt the remaining butter in a small saucepan, then stir in the breadcrumbs and cheese. Remove the cooked gratin from the crock pot and discard the foil. Spoon the cheese mixture over and finish under a preheated grill (broiler) for 3–4 minutes until golden.

Braising red cabbage with fruit is not new, but using pears and walnuts instead of the more usual apple makes it a particularly good accompaniment for gammon, venison sausages or pork chops. Experiment and use white cabbage and white wine vinegar instead of red and you can, of course, take the traditional route and use apples if you prefer!

braised red cabbage with pears and walnuts

SERVES 6–8

1 small red cabbage, shredded
1 onion, thinly sliced
2 slightly under-ripe pears, peeled
   and sliced
A large handful of raisins
50 g/2 oz/½ cup roughly chopped
   walnuts

1 star anise
5 cm/2 in piece of cinnamon stick
Salt and freshly ground black pepper
30 ml/2 tbsp unrefined light brown
   sugar
30 ml/2 tbsp red wine vinegar
45 ml/3 tbsp boiling water

1   Mix the cabbage with the onion, pears, raisins, walnuts, spices, some salt and pepper and the sugar. Tip into the crock pot.

2   Mix together the wine vinegar and boiling water and pour over the cabbage mixture. Cover and cook on High for 2–3 hours or Low for 4–6 hours until tender.

3   Discard the spices, stir and serve.

You will need a large crock pot to get the best results because it is used as a bain marie – a water bath – to gently steam the sponge. Try this dessert with pears instead of apples and you could use maple syrup, which has a lovely smoky flavour, instead or the ordinary golden kind. Ring the changes with ground mixed spice or a tiny pinch of ground cloves instead of cinnamon.

light and luscious apple and syrup sponge

SERVES 6

100 g/4 oz/1 cup self-raising flour
5 ml/1 tsp baking powder
100 g/4 oz/½ cup unrefined light brown sugar
100 g/4 oz/½ cup softened butter or margarine, plus a little extra for greasing
5 ml/1 tsp ground cinnamon
2 eggs
15 ml/1 tbsp milk

2 large cooking (tart) apples, peeled, cored and thinly sliced
45 ml/3 tbsp golden (light corn) syrup
A little unrefined caster (superfine) sugar for sprinkling

TO SERVE:
Cream or custard

1 Put the flour, baking powder, sugar, butter or margarine, cinnamon, eggs and milk in a bowl and beat with a wooden spoon or electric beater just until smooth and fluffy, then stop.

2 Lightly grease a 1.5 litre/2½ pt/6 cup shallow ovenproof dish that will fit in the crock pot. Layer the apple slices in the dish and spoon the syrup over. Cover with the sponge mixture and level the surface.

3 Cover the dish with a dome of greased foil, twisting and folding under the rim to secure (the dome is to allow for the sponge rising).

4 Stand the dish in the crock pot and pour about 2.5 cm/1 in of boiling water around. Cover and cook on High for 2 hours until risen and firm to the touch.

5 Sprinkle with a little caster sugar and serve with cream or custard.

When rhubarb is cooked in a slow cooker on Low it retains its shape, so it looks absolutely lovely, particularly when the pink sticks are mixed with orange slices and flecked with finely shredded orange zest. You can omit the liqueur, but it does add to this dessert to make it taste divine! Try serving the compôte with other luxury sweet biscuits such as macaroons.

rhubarb and orange compôte

SERVES 4

4 oranges
450 g/1 lb forced rhubarb, trimmed
   and cut into short lengths
90 ml/6 tbsp boiling water
75 g/3 oz/⅓ cup unrefined
   granulated sugar

45 ml/3 tbsp Cointreau

TO SERVE:
Amaretti biscuits and vanilla
   ice-cream

1   Thinly pare the zest of one of the oranges and cut it into very thin strips. Hold the oranges one at a time over the crock pot to catch the juice and cut off all the zest and pith. Cut the fruit into slices, discarding any pips, and place in the crock pot.

2   Add the rhubarb to the pot and spread out evenly. Put the shredded zest in a saucepan with the boiling water and bring back to the boil. Stir in the sugar until dissolved and add the Cointreau. Pour over the fruit, cover and cook on Low for 3–4 hours until the rhubarb is really tender.

3   Serve hot or cold with amaretti biscuits and ice-cream.

FEBRUARY

It's mostly greens that are fresh and good this month though there are, of course, plenty of roots and tubers around too. Mussels are superb right now but are not for the slow-cooking treatment; you could, however, steam some in a little white wine or water and throw them in with the papardelle to serve with the Lemon Sole with Pesto on page 25. Now is also the time for good citrus fruits from warmer climes, so look out especially for Seville oranges for making marmalade. I've given you really simple recipe for it on page 30 – there are few things quite so therapeutic as making your own preserves!

Vegetables

Brussels sprouts
Brussels tops
Cabbages (green, red, white)
Carrots
Cauliflowers
Celeriac (celery root)
Celery
Chicory (Belgian endive)
Curly endive (frisée lettuce)
Curly kale
Jerusalem artichokes
Leeks
Lettuces
Onions
Parsnips
Potatoes (old, maincrop)
Rhubarb (forced)
Salad leaves
Salsify and scorzonera
Shallots
Spring (collard) and winter greens
Swedes (rutabaga)
Swiss chard

Fruit and nuts

Apples (Cox's, Bramleys)
Avocados (Fuerte)
Bananas
Blood oranges
Kiwi fruit
Lemons
Mangoes
Oranges
Passion fruit
Pears (Comice)
Pineapple
Pomegranates
Seville oranges

Meat, poultry and game

Guinea fowl
Hare
Venison

Fish and seafood

Brill
Brown shrimp
Clams
Cockles
Cod
Cod's roe
Crabs
Haddock
Hake
Halibut
John Dory
Lemon sole
Mussels
Oysters
Salmon
Turbot

Produce in *italics* is UK seasonal fare at its peak.

I have made many versions of this soup over the years and as slow cooking is the perfect way to make the most of white cabbage I had to include a recipe in this book. I've varied this one by adding some leek and caraway seeds – flavours that only serve to complement this peasant-style dish. Who would have thought that the humble cabbage could be so delicious?

hearty sausage and cabbage soup

SERVES 4

15 g/½ oz/1 tbsp butter
1 onion, chopped
1 leek, thinly sliced
1 celery stick, finely chopped
1 carrot, thinly sliced
250 g/9 oz smoked pork ring, sliced
¼ small white cabbage, shredded
2 potatoes, peeled and cut into
  small dice
1 bay leaf
15 ml/1 tbsp chopped fresh dill (dill
  weed), or 5 ml/1 tsp dried

10 ml/2 tsp caraway seeds
10 ml/2 tsp white wine vinegar
1 litre/1¾ pts/4¼ cups boiling beef
  stock
Salt and freshly ground black pepper
30 ml/2 tbsp chopped fresh parsley
  to garnish

TO SERVE:
Rye bread

1   Melt the butter in a frying pan, add the onion, leek, celery and carrot and fry for 2 minutes, stirring.

2   Add the sausage to the frying pan and cook, stirring, for 1 minute. Tip everything into the crock pot.

3   Add all the remaining ingredients to the crock pot, cover and cook on High for 5 hours or Low for 10 hours.

4   Taste and re-season, if necessary. Discard the bay leaf and serve in warm bowls, garnished with the parsley and plenty of rye bread.

I've used the traditional green basil pesto here, though you could experiment with some of the other ones available, like red, aubergine or coriander. I've suggested a bed of thick ribbon papardelle but you could try another pasta, rice or fluffy mashed potato. If you buy white-skinned lemon sole fillets they won't need skinning as the membrane is very soft when cooked.

lemon sole
with pesto

SERVES 4

25 g/1 oz/2 tbsp unsalted (sweet) butter
60 ml/4 tbsp dry white wine
60 ml/4 tbsp boiling water
Salt and freshly ground black pepper
4 good-sized lemon sole fillets, skinned if the skin is dark
30 ml/2 tbsp green basil pesto from a jar
½ lemon, sliced

350 g/12 oz papardelle
30 ml/2 tbsp freshly grated Parmesan cheese, plus extra to garnish
Wedges of lemon and torn basil leaves to garnish

TO SERVE:
A mixed salad

1   Drop the butter in flakes into the crock pot. Add the wine and boiling water, cover and cook on High for 15 minutes until the butter has melted. Turn the pot to Low.

2   Meanwhile, season the sole lightly, spread with the pesto on the skin sides and roll up.

3   Put the lemon slices in the hot butter and wine mixture and lay the fish in the pot. Turn them over in the hot liquid, then cover the pot and cook on Low for 1 hour until the fillets are cooked through.

4   Meanwhile, cook the papardelle according to the packet directions. Drain.

5   When the fish is cooked, carefully lift it out of the pot with a fish slice, place on a platter and keep warm. Discard the lemon slices. Add the papardelle to the juices in the pot and toss well. Sprinkle in the Parmesan and toss again.

6   Pile the papardelle on to warm plates and place a fish alongside. Garnish with a sprinkling of Parmesan, wedges of lemon and torn basil leaves and serve with a mixed salad.

This dish is a lovely fusion of Cajun and English food. I like to serve it with some finely shredded curly kale, quickly stir-fried in just a splash of oil with some finely grated lemon zest and a crushed garlic clove. When you can't get guinea fowl, you could use chicken portions – which would be almost as delicious! The rub is very versatile and goes well with most meats.

spiced braised guinea fowl with celeriac mash

SERVES 4

FOR THE RUB:
5 ml/1 tsp paprika
5 ml/1 tsp ground cumin
2.5 ml/½ tsp unrefined light brown
   sugar
2.5 ml/½ tsp onion granules
1.5 ml/¼ tsp hot chilli powder
1.5 ml/¼ tsp ground turmeric
1.5 ml/¼ tsp salt
Freshly ground black pepper

TO FINISH:
1 oven-ready guinea fowl, quartered

15 ml/1 tbsp sunflower or groundnut
   (peanut) oil
150 ml/¼ pt/⅔ cup chicken stock

FOR THE CELERIAC MASH:
450 g/1 lb potatoes, peeled and cut
   into chunks
1 small celeriac (celery root), peeled
   and cut into chunks
15 g/½ oz/1 tbsp butter
15 ml/1 tbsp milk
Salt and freshly ground black pepper

1   Mix together all the rub ingredients, including a good grinding of pepper. Rub the guinea fowl all over with the spice rub. Heat the oil in a saucepan, add the guinea fowl and brown quickly on all sides. Transfer to the crock pot.

2   Pour the stock into the saucepan with any remaining rub and bring to the boil, stirring. Pour into the crock pot. Cover and cook on High for 3 hours or Low for 6 hours until the guinea fowl is really tender.

3   When the birds are nearly cooked, boil the potatoes and celeriac in lightly salted water for 15 minutes or until very tender. Drain and return to the saucepan. Heat gently, stirring, to dry them out, then mash well with the butter and milk, seasoning to taste. Keep warm.

4   When the guinea fowl is cooked, transfer the portions to warm plates. Pour the cooking juices into a saucepan and boil rapidly for a minute or two until well reduced and concentrated. Taste and re-season if necessary. Spoon the juices over the guinea fowl and serve with the celeriac mash.

This is a delicious version of a longstanding household favourite. Here pieces of pork are stewed gently in an apple, garlic, tomato and soy sauce sweetened with honey, then shredded seasonal vegetables and fresh pineapple are added just for the last hour or two to created a fabulous-tasting and colourful dish still having all the crunch of a stir-fry.

sweet and sour pork with fresh pineapple

SERVES 4

30 ml/2 tbsp sunflower oil
450 g/1 lb lean boneless belly pork slices, rinded and cut into chunks
200 ml/7 fl oz/scant 1 cup apple juice
90 ml/6 tbsp soy sauce
2 garlic cloves, crushed
15 ml/1 tbsp tomato purée (paste)
10 ml/2 tsp clear honey
2.5 ml/½ tsp Chinese five spice powder
1 small fresh pineapple

2 large carrots, cut into matchsticks
2 celery sticks, cut into matchsticks
1 leek, sliced
¼ small green cabbage, finely shredded
225 g/8 oz/1 small can of bamboo shoots, drained
30 ml/2 tbsp cornflour (cornstarch)
60 ml/4 tbsp water

TO SERVE:
Plain boiled rice

1   Heat the oil in a saucepan, add the pork and brown all over. Transfer to the crock pot with a draining spoon.

2   Bring the apple juice and soy sauce to the boil in the saucepan, then stir in the garlic, tomato purée, honey and spice powder. Add to the pork, cover and cook on High for 2 hours or Low for 4 hours.

3   Meanwhile, cut the green top and all the skin off the pineapple, slice the flesh, then cut it into cubes, discarding any hard central core. Add to the pork with all the vegetables. Stir well, cover and cook on High for a further 1 hour or Low for a further 2 hours.

4   Blend the cornflour with the water and stir into the pot. Cover and cook on High for a further 15 minutes until thickened. Taste and add more soy sauce or a little more honey, if necessary. Serve spooned over rice in bowls.

These make a delicious starter, side dish or lunch and are really simple to make. They have a Greek flavour, so try them topped with some crumbled Feta cheese and a few chopped olives too. It is important to blanch the leaves before stuffing them to ensure they fold and roll easily. Experiment with using other root vegetables when in season.

cabbage leaves stuffed with swede, bulghar and pine nuts

SERVES 4–8

½ small swede (rutabaga), coarsely grated
1 small onion, grated
1 garlic clove, crushed
75 g/3 oz/½ cup bulghar (cracked wheat)
50 g/2 oz/½ cup pine nuts
50 g/2 oz/⅓ cup currants

5 ml/1 tsp dried oregano
2.5 ml/½ tsp ground cinnamon
Salt and freshly ground black pepper
8 large green cabbage leaves
600 ml/1 pt/2½ cups boiling vegetable or chicken stock
45 ml/3 tbsp tomato purée (paste)
2 bay leaves

1   Mix the swede with the onion, garlic, bulghar, pine nuts, currants, oregano and cinnamon. Season well with salt and pepper.

2   Wash the cabbage leaves and cut out the thick central stalks. Plunge the leaves in boiling water for 2 minutes, then drain, rinse with cold water and drain again. Pat the leaves dry on kitchen paper (paper towels).

3   Place equal amounts of the stuffing on each leaf. Fold over the points where the stalks were, then fold in the sides and roll up the leaves fairly loosely (to allow for the bulghar expanding) to form parcels. Pack the parcels side by side in the crock pot (if using a small cooker you will need to pack in two layers with a sheet of non-stick baking parchment between the layers).

4   Mix together the boiling stock and tomato purée and pour over. Tuck the bay leaves between the parcels. Cover and cook on High for 2 hours or Low for 4 hours until cooked through.

5   Discard the bay leaves and serve the cabbage rolls with the cooking juices spooned over.

Mincemeat is most frequently used in mince pies at Christmas, but there is no reason why it can't be enjoyed at other times of the year as well. In this recipe, it adds sweetness and a light spiciness to the pears, and the addition of brandy enhances the flavour no end. However, you could use a little orange liqueur instead of brandy, if you prefer.

pears with brandied mincemeat

SERVES 4–8

4 firm pears
4 heaped tbsp mincemeat
15 ml/1 tbsp brandy
120 ml/4 fl oz/½ cup boiling water
30 ml/2 tbsp unrefined light brown
   sugar

10 ml/2 tsp lemon juice

TO SERVE:
Crème fraîche

1   Peel, halve and core the pears. Cut a thin slice off the rounded side of each half so the halves lie flat. Chop the cut-off slices and mix with the mincemeat and brandy.

2   Lay the pears in the crock pot and spoon the mincemeat mixture into the core cavities.

3   Blend the boiling water with the sugar and lemon juice and pour around. Cover and cook on Low for 2 hours until the pears are tender but still holding their shape.

4   Serve warm or cold with crème fraîche.

Cooking the fruit in the slow cooker first means not only do you ensure wonderfully soft shreds in your finished marmalade and an excellent flavour but you also don't have to worry about boiling them dry – you can leave them to gently soften while you do something else. You can try this recipe with sweet oranges or other citrus when Sevilles aren't around.

seville orange and lemon marmalade

MAKES ABOUT 1.75 KG/4 LB

900 g/2 lb Seville oranges, scrubbed
2 lemons, scrubbed
1 litre/1¾ pts/4¼ cups boiling water

900 g/2 lb unrefined granulated sugar

1 Halve the fruits and squeeze the juices into the crock pot.

2 Quarter the fruits, scrape out the pulp and pips and put these in a muslin (cheesecloth) bag or in a new disposable dish cloth and tie up. Place in the crock pot with the quarters of peel.

3 Add the boiling water, cover and cook on High for 3 hours or Low for 6 hours until the peel is really tender.

4 Strain the liquid into a heavy-based saucepan. Squeeze the bag of pulp and pips against the side of the pan to remove as much juice as possible, then discard.

5 Shred the peel as fine or thick as you like. Add some or all to the pan (depending on how chunky you like you marmalade) with the sugar and heat gently, stirring, until the sugar dissolves. Bring to the boil and boil for about 5 minutes until setting point is reached. To test, dip a wooden spoon into the marmalade. Hold it over the pan on its side and watch the marmalade drip off. If the final drip stays on the edge of the spoon, suspended as jelly, it is set.

6 Pour into clean warm jars, cover, label and leave to cool. Store in a cool, dark place.

MARCH

March is much the same as February but look out for lovely tender purple sprouting broccoli coming in around now. Chicory is good — try it as a vehicle for pâtés, dips and soft cheeses as well as in salads or braised. You'll find the last of the British apples in shops and at market but they will no longer be at their best, though Bramleys and other cookers will still be firm and flavourful. Cockles are still around but, sadly, they don't do well in the slow cooker; they're best eaten freshly steamed with lots of freshly ground black pepper and a splash of vinegar or lemon juice in true seaside fashion!

Vegetables
Cabbages (green)
Carrots
Cauliflowers
Chicory (Belgian endive)
Leeks
Lettuces
Onions
Potatoes (old, maincrop)
Purple sprouting broccoli
Radishes
Rhubarb (forced)
Shallots
Spring (collard) greens
Spring onions (scallions)
Swedes (rutabaga)
Swiss chard

Fruit and nuts
Apples (Cox's, Bramleys)
Avocados (Fuerte)
Bananas
Blood oranges
Kiwi fruit
Lemons
Mangoes
Oranges
Passion fruit
Pineapple
Pomegranates

Meat, poultry and game
Hare

Fish and seafood
Brown shrimp
Cockles
Cod
Hake
John Dory
Mussels
Oysters
Pollack
Salmon
Sea bass
Sea trout

Produce in *italics* is UK seasonal fare at its peak.

This smooth and velvety soup is delicious served with some crusty bread and, if followed by some cold ham, pickles and a side salad it is the perfect starter for a simple meal. It also works well with broccoli instead of cauliflower when in season. For a touch of luxury, add a swirl of double cream to each bowl before sprinkling with the parsley.

cauliflower and stilton soup

SERVES 4

1 small cauliflower
15 g/½ oz/1 tbsp butter
1 onion, chopped
1 large potato, diced
600 ml/1 pt/2½ cups boiling
   vegetable stock
1 bouquet garni sachet

Salt and freshly ground black pepper
100 g/4 oz/1 cup crumbled Stilton
   cheese
300 ml/½ pt/1¼ cups milk
15 ml/1 tbsp chopped fresh parsley
   to garnish

1   Cut the cauliflower into small florets, discarding the green leaves and thick stump. Melt the butter in a saucepan, add the onion and fry, stirring, for 2 minutes until softened but not browned.

2   Tip the onion into the crock pot and add the cauliflower florets, potato, stock, bouquet garni and a little salt and pepper. Cover and cook on High for 2–3 hours or Low for 4–6 hours until really tender.

3   Discard the bouquet garni, then tip the soup into a blender or food processor, add the cheese and milk and run the machine until smooth.

4   Pour the mixture back into to the crock pot, cover and leave on Low to heat through for 5 minutes or until ready to serve.

5   Taste and re-season, if necessary. Ladle into warm bowls and garnish with the chopped parsley.

This is a dish where, if you prefer, you can use two large cans of haricot beans, drained, and start at step 2 instead of starting from scratch. It's worth noting, though, that using dried beans is far cheaper. If you like them and use them a lot, cook double the quantity given in this recipe and store the unused half in the fridge for up to 3 days, or freeze for future use.

hake with harissa
and white beans

SERVES 4

225 g/8 oz/1⅓ cups dried haricot
   (navy) beans, soaked in cold
   water for several hours or
   overnight
2 carrots, diced
30 ml/2 tbsp olive oil
2 onions, chopped
1 garlic clove, crushed
400 g/14 oz/1 large can of chopped
   tomatoes
30 ml/2 tbsp tomato purée (paste)
2 canned red pimiento caps, diced

4 pieces of hake fillet, about 150 g/
   5 oz each, skinned, if preferred
30 ml/2 tbsp harissa paste
1 lemon
Salt and freshly ground black pepper
15 ml/1 tbsp chopped stoned
   (pitted) black and green olives

TO SERVE:
Warm pitta breads and a green salad
   with sliced avocado

1 Drain the beans and place in a saucepan. Cover with cold water, bring to the boil and boil rapidly for 10 minutes.

2 Tip the beans and the cooking liquid into the crock pot and add the carrots. Cover and cook on High for 3 hours or Low for 6 hours until tender. Drain, if necessary, and return to the crock pot.

3 Meanwhile, heat the oil in a large frying pan, add the onions and garlic and fry, stirring, for 2 minutes. Stir in the tomatoes, tomato purée and pimientos and bring to the boil. Stir into the beans.

4 Smear the fish with the harissa paste and place on top. Cut 2 slices from the lemon and tuck them in around the fish. Season, cover and cook on Low for 1 hour until the fish is tender.

5 Discard the lemon slices. Serve the dish straight from the pot, garnished with the chopped olives and the remaining lemon cut into wedges, with warm pitta breads and a green salad with avocado.

If you make fish pie the conventional way, simmering the fish first in a saucepan then thickening it, the fish tends to break up. Making it in the slow cooker ensures a perfect texture and the bonus of no pan to clean. So this is a simple, perfect and utterly delicious fish pie that is very easy to make. Use any fish in season. You need a large slow cooker for this.

easy steps
fish pie

SERVES 4

150 ml/¼ pt/⅔ cup dry white wine
150 ml/¼ pt/⅔ cup crème fraîche
45 ml/3 tbsp cornflour (cornstarch)
4 mushrooms, sliced
4 spring onions (scallions), finely chopped
1 bouquet garni sachet
Salt and freshly ground black pepper
1 piece of salmon fillet, about 350 g/ 12 oz, skinned and cut into chunks
1 piece of smoked cod fillet, about 175 g/6 oz, skinned and cut into chunks

1 piece of pollack fillet, about 225 g/8 oz, skinned and cut into chunks
30 ml/2 tbsp chopped fresh parsley
700 g/1½ lb potatoes, scrubbed and sliced
A good knob of butter
30 ml/2 tbsp grated Cheddar cheese

TO SERVE:
Purple sprouting broccoli

1 Blend the wine with the crème fraîche and cornflour in a shallow flameproof dish that will fit in a large slow cooker. Stir in the mushrooms and spring onions, add the bouquet garni and season to taste.

2 Pour about 2.5 cm/1 in of boiling water around the dish, cover and cook on Low for 2 hours.

3 Stir the sauce well and discard the bouquet garni. Gently fold in all the fish, add the parsley, re-cover and cook on Low for a further 1 hour until all the fish is cooked.

4 Meanwhile, cook the potato slices in boiling, lightly salted water for about 6–8 minutes until just tender but still holding their shape, Drain thoroughly.

5 Lift the dish out of the slow cooker, taste and re-season, if necessary. Arrange the potatoe slices over the fish and dot with the butter. Sprinkle with the cheese, then place under a preheated moderate grill (broiler) for about 5 minutes until golden brown. Serve with purple sprouting broccoli.

Yes, I know I've cheated because the chicory isn't cooked in the slow cooker, but this is such a perfect slow-cooked recipe that I just had to include it. The potted meat can also be used in sandwiches. It will keep for several days in the fridge but, to preserve it longer, cover it in a layer of melted butter, which once set will seal it completely.

potted beef with carrots on chicory

SERVES 6

500 g/18 oz lean stewing steak, diced	20 ml/4 tsp anchovy essence (extract)
2 carrots, chopped	60 ml/4 tbsp boiling water
1 onion, chopped	100 g/4 oz/½ cup unsalted (sweet)
A good grating of nutmeg	butter, thinly sliced
A good grinding of black pepper	3 heads of chicory (Belgian endive)
1 bay leaf	Sliced cornichons to garnish

1 Put the steak in the crock pot and add the carrots, onion, nutmeg, pepper, bay leaf and anchovy essence. Stir in the boiling water and dot the slices of butter all over the surface. Cover and cook on Low for 8 hours.

2 Discard the bay leaf, tip into a food processor and blend until smooth. Taste and re-season, if necessary. Turn into a sealable plastic container, cover and leave to cool, then chill for at least 2 hours until firm. It can be stored in the fridge for several days.

3 When ready to serve, cut a cone shape out of the bitter-tasting base of each head of chicory. Separate the heads into leaves, then fill with the potted meat. Garnish with sliced cornichons and serve.

Lemons are good at this time of year so I've included this recipe here. Try to use organic garlic; it's always available and the English varieties will be in season by next month so buy it when you can! The chunks of roasted lemon and garlic add a wonderful deep flavour – much more intense than just adding lemon juice and a crushed garlic clove.

lemon chicken with garlic and thyme

SERVES 4

15 g/½ oz/1 tbsp butter
15 ml/1 tbsp olive oil
1 oven-ready chicken, about
   1.5 kg/3 lb, cut into 8 pieces
2 unwaxed lemons, cut into eighths,
   pips removed
1 head of garlic, separated into
   cloves and peeled

30 ml/2 tbsp clear honey
90 ml/6 tbsp dry white wine
30 ml/2 tbsp chopped fresh thyme
Salt and freshly ground black pepper

TO SERVE:
Sauté potatoes and purple sprouting
   broccoli

1 Heat the butter and oil in a frying pan, add the chicken pieces and brown them on all sides. Transfer the chicken to the crock pot with a draining spoon.

2 Add the lemon chunks and garlic cloves to the frying pan and fry, stirring, for 2 minutes until browning slightly. Add to the chicken.

3 Add the honey and wine to the pan and bring to the boil, stirring. Pour all over the chicken, lemons and garlic, sprinkle with the thyme and season well. Cover and cook on High for 2–3 hours or Low for 4–6 hours until the chicken is really tender.

4 Taste and re-season, if necessary. Serve with sauté potatoes and purple sprouting broccoli.

Not a British recipe at all, but as Thai food has become one of the most popular cuisines, I thought I'd include it. I love the thinner consistency of Thai curries and the way the hotness of the chilli doesn't linger when you've finished eating. You can try using some lightly cooked green beans when in season instead of cauliflower.

thai red beef and cauliflower curry

SERVES 4

30 ml/2 tbsp sunflower oil

2 garlic cloves, crushed

1 onion, roughly chopped

700 g/1½ lb braising steak, cut into large cubes

2 large potatoes, peeled and cut into fairly large chunks

45 ml/3 tbsp Thai red curry paste

5 ml/1 tsp unrefined caster (superfine) sugar

400 g/14 oz/1 large can of coconut milk

Salt and freshly ground black pepper

2 thin red chillies, halved lengthways and seeded, if preferred

½ small cauliflower, cut into small florets

50 g/2 oz/½ cup raw cashew nuts

4 tomatoes, quartered

A few coriander (cilantro) leaves and wedges of lemon to garnish

TO SERVE:

Thai jasmine rice

1 Heat the oil in a frying pan. Add the garlic, onion and meat and cook, stirring and turning, for about 3 minutes until the meat is browned. Transfer to the crock pot and add the potatoes.

2 Blend the curry paste with the sugar and coconut milk in the frying pan. Season to taste. Bring to the boil and pour over the meat, then scatter the chillies over. Cover and cook on High for 4–5 hours or Low for 8–10 hours until the meat is really tender.

3 Meanwhile, blanch the cauliflower florets in boiling water for 2 minutes, then drain. Add the cauliflower, nuts and tomatoes to the curry, pushing them down well into the sauce, cover and cook on High for a further 30 minutes.

4 Serve spooned over jasmine rice in bowls and garnish each serving with a few coriander leaves and a wedge of lemon.

There aren't many side dishes in this book but this delicious one had to be included. It's so good for you, not least because the cooking water is used in the final dish so most of the nutrients are retained. Traditionally, champ is just potatoes and spring onions, but my version with swede is the perfect accompaniment to grilled gammon, sausages or liver.

swede and sesame seed champ

SERVES 4

1 small swede (rutabaga), diced
2 potatoes, diced
1 bunch of spring onions (scallions), chopped
150 ml/¼ pt/⅔ cup boiling water

Salt and freshly ground black pepper
60 ml/4 tbsp dried milk powder (non-fat dry milk)
30 ml/2 tbsp toasted sesame seeds
50 g/2 oz/¼ cup butter, melted

1   Put the swede and potatoes in the crock pot. Reserve a little of the chopped spring onions for garnish and put the remainder in the pot. Add the boiling water and some salt and pepper, then cover and cook on High for 3 hours or Low for 6 hours until the vegetables are really tender.

2   Sprinkle in the milk powder and mash well. Taste and re-season, if necessary.

3   Pile the champ on to warm plates and make a slight well in the centre of each pile. Sprinkle all over with the sesame seeds and pour the melted butter into the wells. Garnish with the reserved spring onion and serve.

*Blood oranges are always a wonder to me. You never know just how
flecked with red the fruit will be until you cut them open. They are usually
very sweet and juicy, though, and perfect for these orange creams. You'll
certainly be packing in the vitamin C with the fragrant kiwi fruit coulis
too! You can substitute ordinary oranges, if necessary.*

blood orange creams
with kiwi coulis

SERVES 4

A little sunflower oil for greasing
2 blood oranges
300 ml/½ pt/1¼ cups crème fraîche
2 eggs
50 g/2 oz/¼ cup unrefined caster
   (superfine) sugar

2 kiwi fruit
30 ml/2 tbsp icing (confectioners')
   sugar, sifted

1 Lightly oil four ramekins (custard cups). Thinly pare the zest from
one of the oranges and cut it into thin strips. Boil in water for
2 minutes, then drain, rinse with cold water and drain again.
Reserve for decoration.

2 Grate the zest from the second orange and squeeze the juice from
both oranges into a bowl.

3 Whisk the grated orange zest, crème fraîche, eggs and caster
sugar into the orange juice, then pour into the ramekins.

4 Stand the ramekins in the crock pot and pour in enough boiling
water to come half-way up the sides of the dishes. Cover and cook
on Low for 2–3 hours until set.

5 Remove from the crock pot, leave to cool, then chill.

6 Meanwhile cut a thin slice off the top of each kiwi fruit and scoop
out the flesh into a bowl with a teaspoon. Purée with a hand
blender or pass through a sieve (strainer). Stir in the icing sugar.

7 Spoon the kiwi coulis on top of the creams, leaving a small border
of the orange cream showing all round. Top with the shredded
orange zest and serve.

APRIL

Cauliflowers are great now – large, firm and white. My favourite green vegetable – spinach – will be coming into its own, too. I love it as a bed for numerous dishes based on fish, eggs, meat or poultry. You'll find it as a serving suggestion on many occasions throughout this book when it's in season and I've included a delicious soup recipe on page 42. It's also the time for morel mushrooms – but they can be elusive creatures! Enjoy them this month or next whenever you can find them. Sauté them in butter and serve on toast or you could use them, mixed with some cultivated mushrooms, for wild mushroom soup (you'll find the recipe in the October chapter as that's when other wild mushrooms are available).

Vegetables
Broccoli (calabrese)
Cabbages (green)
Carrots
Cauliflowers
Garlic
Horseradish
Jersey Royal new
   potatoes
Lettuces
Morel mushrooms
Purple sprouting broccoli
Radishes
Rhubarb
Rocket (arugula)
Sorrel
Spinach
Spring (collard) greens
Spring onions (scallions)
Watercress

Fruit and nuts
Avocados (Fuerte, Hass)
Bananas
Kiwi fruit
Loquats
Mangoes
Muscat grapes

Meat, poultry and game
Lamb
Poussins (Cornish hens)
Rabbit
Wood pigeon

Fish and seafood
Brown shrimp
Cockles
Cod
Crabs
Dublin bay prawns
   (scampi)
Halibut
John Dory
Salmon
Sea bass
Sea trout

Produce in *italics* is UK seasonal fare at its peak.

Watercress has many health-giving properties but is far too often overlooked, perhaps because its peppery flavour is an acquired taste. Try it in sandwiches made with fresh crusty bread, and you'll love it in this elegant soup, which is perfect for a light lunch or as a starter for a special occasion meal. You could use an egg poacher to cook the eggs.

watercress soup
with poached eggs

SERVES 4

15 g/½ oz/1 tbsp butter
1 onion, chopped
1 large potato, diced
1 bunch of watercress, about
    100 g/4 oz
600 ml/1 pt/2½ cups boiling chicken
    or vegetable stock

15 ml/1 tbsp chopped fresh thyme
30 ml/2 tbsp chopped fresh parsley
Salt and freshly ground black pepper
120 ml/4 fl oz/½ cup single (light)
    cream
4 eggs
15 ml/1 tbsp lemon juice

1   Melt the butter in a saucepan, add the onion and fry, stirring, for 2 minutes until it is softened but not browned. Stir in the potato, then tip everything into the crock pot.

2   Add the watercress, stock, thyme, half the parsley and some salt and pepper. Cover and cook on High for 2 hours or Low for 4 hours.

3   Purée the soup in a blender or food processor with the cream, then return it to the crock pot. Taste and re-season if necessary. Leave on Low until ready to serve.

4   When ready to serve, poach the eggs in gently simmering water with the lemon juice added until cooked to your liking.

5   As soon as the eggs are just about ready, ladle the soup into warm open soup plates and gently lay a poached egg in each plate of soup. Sprinkle with the remaining parsley and serve.

This soup is thick, smooth and luscious. If you prefer, you could use a large can of butter beans instead of dried and start at step 2. Spinach and nutmeg are natural flavour partners but, rather than buying a jar of ready-grated, it's worth buying a whole nutmeg, which will keep for ages, and finely grating off the amount you need each time.

spinach and butter bean soup

SERVES 4

100 g/4 oz butter (lima) beans, soaked in cold water for several hours or overnight
2 spring onions (scallions), chopped
1 large potato, diced
350 g/12 oz fresh spinach, thoroughly washed and roughly chopped

2.5 ml/½ tsp dried mixed herbs
Salt and freshly ground black pepper
A good grating of fresh nutmeg
About 750 ml/1¼ pts/3 cups boiling chicken or vegetable stock
120 ml/4 fl oz/½ cup single (light) cream or milk

1 Drain the beans, place in a saucepan and just cover with fresh water. Bring to the boil and boil rapidly for 10 minutes. Turn down the heat and simmer for 45 minutes until almost tender. Drain off the cooking liquid into a measuring jug and tip the beans into the crock pot. Add all the remaining ingredients except the stock and cream or milk.

2 Make up the cooking liquid to 900 ml/1½ pt/3¾ cups with boiling stock. Pour into the crock pot, cover and cook on High for 2–3 hours or Low for 4–6 hours until everything is really tender.

3 Purée the soup in a blender or food processor with the cream or milk. Taste and re-season with more nutmeg, salt and pepper, if necessary. Return to the crock pot on Low until ready to serve.

I like cooking with rosé wine as I find it tends to have a slightly fruitier flavour than most white wines. The pink colour doesn't come through very much in the finished sauce – and there's also the advantage that the rest of the bottle is the perfect accompaniment to drink with it. So don't forget to keep it chilling in the fridge while the fish is cooking!

salmon in creamy rosé wine and butter sauce

SERVES 4

4 thick pieces of salmon fillet, about
   150 g/5 oz each
1 bay leaf
6 whole black peppercorns
1 onion, halved
150 ml/¼ pt/⅔ cup dry rosé wine
60 ml/4 tbsp water
15 ml/1 tbsp brandy

50 g/2 oz/¼ cup unsalted (sweet)
   butter, cut into small pieces
75 ml/5 tbsp double (heavy) cream
Salt and white pepper
Sprigs of watercress to garnish

TO SERVE:
Plain boiled rice

1 Lay the fish in the crock pot and add the bay leaf, whole peppercorns and onion.

2 Bring the wine, water and brandy to the boil in a small saucepan and add to the pot. Cover and poach on Low for 1 hour.

3 Carefully strain off the cooking juices into the saucepan. Turn off the slow cooker and leave the salmon in it, covered, to keep warm.

4 Bring the juices to the boil and boil rapidly until syrupy and reduced by half. Turn the heat down and gradually whisk in the butter a piece at a time until the sauce has thickened slightly. Whisk in the cream and season to taste with salt and white pepper.

5 Transfer the fish to warm plates and spoon the butter sauce over. Garnish with sprigs of watercress and serve with rice.

Watercress makes a great sauce to serve with any fish, particularly the oily varieties such as salmon or, as here, sea trout. It has a lovely velvety texture and its pale colour is just delicately flecked with the fresh green of the watercress. The sauce is also delicious spooned over poached eggs on toast, then flashed under a hot grill to glaze the tops.

sea trout fillets
with watercress sauce

SERVES 4

4 sea trout fillets, about 175 g/6 oz each
6 whole black peppercorns
1 bay leaf
Salt and freshly ground black pepper
90 ml/6 tbsp dry white wine
90 ml/6 tbsp water

FOR THE SAUCE:
1 bunch of watercress, about 100 g/4 oz

About 60 ml/4 tbsp double (heavy) cream
45 ml/3 tbsp plain (all-purpose) flour
150 ml/¼ pt/⅔ cup milk
A good knob of butter

TO SERVE:
Fluffy mashed potatoes and carrots

1 Lay the trout fillets side by side in the crock pot. Add the whole peppercorns, the bay leaf and a pinch of salt.

2 Bring the wine and water to the boil in a small saucepan and pour over the fish. Cover and cook on Low for 1 hour.

3 Meanwhile, to make the sauce, reserve 4 small sprigs of watercress for garnish and chop the remainder, discarding the feathery stalks.

4 When the fish is cooked, turn off the cooker and carefully strain off the cooking liquid into a measuring jug. Leave the fish in the slow cooker, covered, to keep warm.

5 Make up the cooking liquid to 150 ml/¼ pt/⅔ cup with the cream.

6 Whisk together the flour and milk in the saucepan. Blend in the stock and cream. Add the butter, bring to the boil and cook for 2 minutes, whisking all the time, until thickened and smooth. Stir in the chopped watercress and season to taste.

7 Transfer the fish to warm plates with a fish slice. Spoon the sauce over and garnish with the reserved sprigs of watercress. Serve with mashed potatoes and carrots.

This delicious Spanish-style omelette is slow-baked rather than fried, but using the High setting for cooking the eggs emulates frying. It's ideal for a light lunch when served with a salad, but it could also be a starter for eight people. Use a mandolin, if you have one, to slice the potatoes. Instead of the crab dressing, you could serve the tortilla on some warm passata.

warm tortilla
with fresh crab dressing

SERVES 4

90 ml/6 tbsp olive oil
2 onions, thinly sliced
4 large potatoes, peeled and very
   thinly sliced
6 eggs
Salt and freshly ground black pepper

FOR THE DRESSING:
60 ml/4 tbsp mayonnaise
30 ml/2 tbsp sunflower oil

15 ml/1 tbsp lemon juice
60 ml/4 tbsp milk
15 ml/1 tbsp tomato purée (paste)
100 g/4 oz fresh white crabmeat
40 g/1½ oz/1 small can of dressed
   crab
30 ml/2 tbsp chopped fresh parsley
   to garnish

1   Brush the crock pot with a little of the oil. Heat the remaining oil in a saucepan, add the onions and fry, stirring, for 2 minutes.

2   Add the potatoes and toss well. Cook for a further 2 minutes, stirring, then tip the whole lot into the crock pot (keep the saucepan for making the salsa). Spread out the mixture as evenly as possible, then cover and cook on High for 1–2 hours until the potatoes are really tender.

3   Beat the eggs with some salt and pepper and pour into the pot. Stir well, then cover and cook for 30 minutes until set.

4   Meanwhile, to make the dressing, mix together all the ingredients and season to taste.

5   When the tortilla is cooked, remove the crock pot from the base and leave the tortilla to cool for 10 minutes before cutting it into wedges. Spoon the dressing on to plates and spread it out. Place one or two wedges of tortilla on top (if using two, put them at a jaunty angle one on top of the other). Sprinkle with the parsley and serve.

In this two-stage dish, the pigeons are slow-cooked with vegetables in a rich wine sauce, making the meat tender and tasty. It is then taken off the bones, the sauce is thickened and the dish is topped with pastry. You could prepare the pie one day, letting the filling cool completely before topping with the pastry, then chill it ready to bake the next day.

pigeon and potato pie

SERVES 4

2 large potatoes, cut into bite-sized pieces
2 large carrots, sliced
2 oven-ready pigeons, halved
15 g/½ oz/1 tbsp butter
50 g/2 oz unsmoked lardons (diced bacon)
2 onions, chopped
150 ml/¼ pt/⅔ cup chicken stock
150 ml/¼ pt/⅔ cup red wine
15 ml/1 tbsp redcurrant jelly (clear conserve)
10 ml/2 tsp tomato purée (paste)
5 ml/1 tsp anchovy essence (extract)
Salt and freshly ground black pepper
1 bay leaf
45 ml/3 tbsp cornflour (cornstarch)
45 ml/3 tbsp water
350 g/12 oz puff pastry (paste), thawed if frozen
15 ml/1 tbsp double (heavy) or single (light) cream

TO SERVE:
Shredded greens

1   Put the potatoes and carrots in the crock pot. Rinse the pigeon halves under cold running water and pat dry on kitchen paper (paper towels).

2   Heat the butter in a frying pan, add the pigeons and brown all over. Remove the pigeons with a draining spoon and place in the crock pot.

3   Add the lardons and onions to the frying pan and fry, stirring, for 2 minutes until golden brown. Transfer to the crock pot.

4   Add the stock, wine, redcurrant jelly, tomato purée and anchovy essence to the pan and bring to the boil, stirring. Season to taste, pour into the pot and add the bay leaf. Cover and cook on High for 3 hours or Low for 6 hours until the pigeons and vegetables are tender.

5 Lift the pigeons out of the pot and place on a board. Lift out the vegetables and lardons with a draining spoon and transfer to a 1.2 litre/2 pt/5 cup pie dish.

6 Remove all the meat from the pigeons with a sharp knife (it will feel quite firm). Cut it into neat pieces and add to the pie dish.

7 Blend the cornflour with the water and stir into the cooking juices. Stir well, then taste and re-season, if necessary. Discard the bay leaf and pour the sauce over the meat and vegetables.

8 Roll out the pastry to just larger than the pie dish and cut a strip off the edge. Dampen the rim of the pie dish and lay the strip around the rim. Dampen the strip with water again and top with the remaining pastry, trimming it to fit. Make a hole in the centre to allow steam to escape. Make leaves out of trimmings and arrange them on top of the pie. Brush the pastry with the cream to glaze.

9 Preheat the oven to 220°C/425°F/gas 7/fan oven 200°C. Bake in the centre of the oven for about 30 minutes until risen, golden and hot through. Serve with shredded greens.

At one time poussins were known as 'spring chickens' but probably because they are now farmed all the year round the name seems to have dropped out of use. Despite their constant availability, they are still the perfect seasonal dish, gently cooked with baby new potatoes and with the rich, enticing flavours of fragrant rosemary, citrus and salty, creamy olives.

honey-glazed poussins with rosemary, baby new potatoes and olives

SERVES 4

2 sprigs of fresh rosemary
30 ml/2 tbsp finely chopped stoned (pitted) green olives
Finely grated zest and juice of ½ lemon
15 g/½ oz/1 tbsp softened butter
Freshly ground black pepper
2 poussins (Cornish hens), halved

30 ml/2 tbsp olive oil
16–20 baby new potatoes, scrubbed
30 ml/2 tbsp clear honey
150 ml/¼ pt/⅔ cup chicken stock
Coarse sea salt

TO SERVE:
Broccoli

1 Strip the rosemary leaves off their stalks and chop finely. Mix with the olives, lemon zest, butter and some black pepper.

2 Loosen the skin on the poussins and smear the olive mixture between the skin and the flesh.

3 Heat the oil in a frying pan, add the poussins and brown quickly on all sides. Put the potatoes in the crock pot and lay the poussin halves, skin-sides up, on top.

4 Mix the honey with the lemon juice and smear all over the birds. Pour the stock into the frying pan and bring to the boil, stirring. Pour around the birds. Cover and cook on High for 2 hours or Low for 4 hours until the potatoes and poussins are tender.

5 Carefully transfer the birds and potatoes to warm plates and keep warm. Pour the juices into a small saucepan and boil rapidly for a few minutes until reduced and slightly thickened. Pour over the birds and sprinkle with a few grains of coarse sea salt. Serve with broccoli.

This is a rich and delicious dessert, reminiscent of nursery days. It's so quick and simple to prepare and can be left to cook for several hours without spoiling. I've finished the dish with a little strawberry jam to enhance its appearance but you could use raspberry or any other jam, if you prefer, or even omit the jam, and the toasted coconut, altogether.

baked
banana custard

SERVES 4–6

2 bananas, thickly sliced
300 ml/½ pt/1¼ cups milk
150 ml/¼ pt/⅔ cup single (light)
   cream
2 eggs
40 g/1½ oz/3 tbsp unrefined caster
   (superfine) sugar

½ vanilla pod
A little oil for greasing
60 ml/4 tbsp strawberry jam
   (conserve)
45 ml/3 tbsp toasted desiccated
   (shredded) coconut

1   Put the bananas in a blender or food processor with the milk, cream, eggs and sugar. Split the vanilla pod and scrape the seeds into the mixture. Cover and blend until smooth.

2   Pour into a lightly greased 18 cm/7 in soufflé dish. Cover with foil, twisting and folding under the rim to secure. Place the dish in the crock pot and pour round enough boiling water to come half-way up the sides of the dish. Cover and cook on Low for 3 hours until the custard is set.

3   Remove the dish from the slow cooker and leave to cool.

4   Spread with the jam and sprinkle with the coconut, then chill until ready to serve.

MAY

My favourite vegetable arrives! Asparagus will be available around now – those gorgeous shoots of sheer pleasure. It slow cooks very well because when you boil it the heads are liable to drop off, which they don't when gently cooked in just a little liquid. Baby broad beans also like the slow-cooked treatment and you must make the most of wonderful, earthy Jersey Royal new potatoes. You may also find the first sweet British cherry tomatoes. Buy them on the vine, if you can, because they will have more flavour and fragrance.

Vegetables

Asparagus
Broad (fava) beans
Broccoli (calabrese)
Carrots
Cauliflowers
Cucumbers
Globe artichokes
Jersey Royal new
*   potatoes*
Lettuces
Morel mushrooms
New potatoes
Peas
Radishes
Rhubarb
Rocket (arugula)
Sorrel
Spinach
Spring onions (scallions)
Watercress

Fruit and nuts

Avocados (Fuerte, Hass)
Bananas
Cherry tomatoes
Elderflowers
Kiwi fruit
Lychees
Mangoes

Meat, poultry and game

Lamb
Wood pigeon

Fish and seafood

Bream
Brown shrimp
Cod
Crabs
Crayfish
Dublin bay prawns
*   (scampi)*
Dover sole
Halibut
John Dory
Pollack
Prawns
River trout (brown,
    rainbow)
Salmon
Sea bass
Sea trout

Produce in *italics* is UK seasonal fare at its peak.

This lovely pale green, smooth, distinctly English soup is equally delicious served hot or chilled. Sorrel, also known as 'spinach dock', is a cross between a herb and a vegetable and has been cultivated for centuries. Its delicate lemony flavour is delicious in soup; however, if you don't like it or can't find it, you could just add extra lettuce leaves.

sorrel and lettuce soup

SERVES 4

1 round lettuce, shredded
100 g/4 oz sorrel, shredded
25 g/1 oz/2 tbsp butter
1 onion, finely chopped
1 large potato, diced
1 litre/1¾ pts/4¼ cups chicken or
   vegetable stock

5 ml/1 tsp chopped fresh thyme
Salt and freshly ground black pepper
A good pinch of grated nutmeg
75 ml/5 tbsp double (heavy) cream
15 ml/1 tbsp chopped fresh parsley
   to garnish

1 Put the lettuce and sorrel in the crock pot.

2 Melt the butter in a saucepan. Add the onion and potato and fry gently, stirring, for 2 minutes until softened but not browned.

3 Add the stock, thyme and a little salt and pepper to the saucepan, bring to the boil, then pour into the crock pot. Cover and cook on High for 2 hours or Low for 4 hours until everything is tender.

4 Purée the mixture in a blender or food processor, then rub it through a sieve (strainer). Stir in the nutmeg and 60 ml/4 tbsp of the cream. If wishing to serve the soup hot, return it to the crock pot, cover and reheat on High for 10 minutes. If you want to serve it chilled, pour into a sealable container, allow to cool, then chill.

5 When ready to serve, ladle into soup cups and garnish each with a swirl of the remaining cream and a little of the parsley.

This is a lovely starter, though it could also serve four people as a light lunch. It's a quick dish by slow-cooker standards but it does save juggling with pans and a hot grill. Be warned, though, that it isn't a dish to leave sitting in the crock pot once cooked because the Camembert would run and the tomatoes would fall apart. You will need to use a large cooker.

warm balsamic vine cherry tomatoes and somerset camembert with rocket

SERVES 6

6 sprigs of cherry tomatoes on the vine, each with about 6 tomatoes
1 firm Somerset Camembert, chilled and cut into 6 wedges
15 ml/1 tbsp unrefined caster (superfine) sugar
45 ml/3 tbsp balsamic vinegar

30 ml/2 tbsp olive oil
Salt and freshly ground black pepper
6 good handfuls of rocket (arugula)

TO SERVE:
Crusty bread

1 Put two pieces of oiled foil side by side in the crock pot. Turn up the edges all round each piece to form containers that won't allow the water around to seep in. Lay the sprigs of tomatoes on one piece and put the Camembert wedges on the other.

2 Mix together the sugar, balsamic vinegar, oil, a pinch of salt and lots of pepper and spoon over the tomatoes.

3 Carefully pour enough boiling water round the sides of the foil containers to just cover no more than the base, taking care that none gets into the foil containers. Cover and cook on Low for 1 hour until the tomatoes are hot but still hold their shape and the cheese is beginning to run.

4 Lift the foil containers out of the slow cooker. Put a pile of rocket to one side of six small serving plates. Transfer the tomatoes to the rocket and spoon the dressing over. Lay a piece of Camembert to one side of each and serve straight away with crusty bread.

Slow-cooking asparagus means you don't have the problem of the heads falling off, which happens only too often when you boil it in water. For quickness, if you prefer (particularly if you like runny eggs), rather than using the slow cooker, you could poach the eggs in a pan of water with a dash of lemon juice added or in an egg poacher.

asparagus with coddled eggs and fresh herb balsamic dressing

SERVES 4

450 g/1 lb asparagus, trimmed
150 ml/¼ pt/⅔ cup boiling water
Salt and freshly ground black pepper
4 eggs

FOR THE DRESSING:
60 ml/4 tbsp olive oil

30 ml/2 tbsp white balsamic
  condiment
15 ml/1 tbsp chopped fresh parsley
15 ml/1 tbsp chopped fresh thyme

1 Lay the asparagus in the crock pot in an even layer. Add the boiling water and a pinch of salt. Cover and cook on High for 1 hour.

2 Lift the asparagus out of the crock pot with a fish slice, transfer to a warm plate and cover with foil to keep warm or leave to cool, as you prefer.

3 Gently break the eggs into the asparagus cooking water. Turn down the heat to Low, cover and cook for 12–15 minutes until the eggs are just set but the yolks are not completely firm.

4 Meanwhile, whisk together the oil and balsamic condiment, then whisk in the herbs and a little salt and pepper.

5 Transfer the asparagus to warm individual plates. Whisk the dressing again and spoon over and around. Lift out the eggs with a draining spoon and arrange on the asparagus portions. Serve straight away.

It's good to have a mixture of oily and white fish in this delicately flavoured stew, such as salmon, pollack and John Dory. You can add other seafood in season, too, like prawns, scallops or crayfish tails. For colour, I sometimes throw in a handful of thawed frozen peas for the last few minutes' cooking time. As you can see, the preparation could hardly be simpler.

mixed fish and new potato stew with saffron

SERVES 4

15 g/½ oz/1 tbsp butter
1 bunch of spring onions (scallions), chopped
350 g/12 oz baby Jersey Royal potatoes, scrubbed
2 carrots, sliced
1 bouquet garni sachet
Salt and freshly ground black pepper

450 ml/¾ pt/2 cups fish or chicken stock
1.5 ml/¼ tsp saffron strands
700 g/1½ lb mixed fish fillets in season, cut into chunks
A little chopped fresh parsley to garnish

1 Melt the butter in a saucepan, add the spring onions and fry, stirring, for 1 minute. Tip into the crock pot and add the potatoes, carrots and bouquet garni. Season with salt and pepper.

2 Pour the stock into the saucepan with the saffron and bring to the boil. Add to the crock pot, cover and cook on High for 2 hours or Low for 4 hours.

3 Add the fish, cover and cook for a further 1 hour on Low.

4 Season to taste and serve in bowls, garnished with parsley.

Halibut is one of my favourite fish, being both meaty and succulent. Here I've gently poached it to serve warm with a cold relish piled on top – almost a warm salad really. You could also add a tomato side salad if you wish. Use a good-quality bought mayonnaise to dress the new potatoes – or why not make your own with the time saved by using the slow cooker?

poached halibut with cucumber and caper salpiçon

SERVES 4

4 thick pieces of halibut fillet, about 150 g/5 oz each
Salt and freshly ground black pepper
120 ml/4 fl oz/½ cup cider
120 ml/4 fl oz/½ cup water
½ cucumber, coarsely grated
15 ml/1 tbsp pickled capers, chopped

30 ml/2 tbsp chopped fresh dill (dill weed)
15 ml/1 tbsp white balsamic condiment

TO SERVE:
Warm new potatoes dressed with mayonnaise

1 Put the halibut in the crock pot and season well.

2 Bring the cider and water to the boil in a saucepan and pour around the fish. Cover and cook on Low for 1 hour.

3 Meanwhile, squeeze the grated cucumber to remove excess moisture. Mix with the capers, dill and balsamic condiment.

4 When the fish is cooked, lift it out of the poaching liquid and transfer to warm plates. Top with the cucumber salpiçon and serve with warm new potatoes dressed with mayonnaise.

This lovely combination is based on a Vietnamese speciality, which despite using ingredients of the late spring season has a deliciously warm and comforting feel. The combination of sweet and hot spices adds depth of flavour. For added colour and nutrients, add some blanched broccoli florets at the end of cooking. Cooked radishes taste like tiny turnips!

spicy beef steak with baby vegetables

SERVES 4

1 bunch of spring onions (scallions), cut into short lengths
2 garlic cloves, finely chopped
½ bunch of radishes, trimmed
100 g/4 oz baby carrots, trimmed, and halved if long
100 g/4 oz shelled baby broad (fava) beans
350 g/12 oz baby new potatoes, scrubbed
15 ml/1 tbsp grapeseed or sunflower oil
4 beef frying steaks, about 100–175 g/4–6 oz each
5 ml/1 tsp mild curry powder

10 ml/2 tsp grated fresh root ginger
5 cm/2 in piece of cinnamon stick
2 star anise
1 fat red chilli, seeded and chopped
1 fat green chilli, seeded and chopped
1 bay leaf
30 ml/2 tbsp tomato purée (paste)
5 ml/1 tsp clear honey
200 ml/7 fl oz/scant 1 cup boiling beef stock
Salt and freshly ground black pepper
30 ml/2 tbsp chopped fresh coriander (cilantro) or parsley

1 Put the prepared vegetables in the crock pot.

2 Heat the oil in a frying pan, add the beef and fry quickly on both sides to brown. Place on top of the vegetables.

3 Add the curry powder, spices, chillies, bay leaf, tomato purée, honey and stock to the pan and bring to the boil, stirring. Pour into the crock pot, season, cover and cook on High for 4 hours or Low for 8 hours.

4 Discard the bay leaf, cinnamon stick and star anise, taste and re-season if necessary. Serve in large open soup bowls, garnished with the coriander or parsley.

Mangoes are at their best now so I felt I just had to include a mango-based dessert in this book. You could experiment with using other soft fruits – strawberries, raspberries or peaches could all be given the same treatment and would give excellent results. When passion fruit are in season, scoop the pulp from one into the mango before pureeing.

hot mango
mousse

SERVES 4

1 large ripe mango
30 ml/2 tbsp lime juice
2 eggs, separated
75 g/3 oz/⅓ cup unrefined caster
  (superfine) sugar
A little sunflower oil for greasing

A little icing (confectioners') sugar,
  sifted

TO SERVE:
Cream and amaretti biscuits

1   Peel the mango and cut all the flesh off the stone (pit). Purée with the lime juice.

2   Whisk the egg whites in a bowl until stiff. Whisk the caster sugar and egg yolks in another bowl until thick and pale. Fold the yolks and sugar into the mango purée, then fold in the egg whites.

3   Spoon into four lightly oiled ramekins (custard cups). Place in the crock pot, cover and cook on Low for 2 hours until risen and set.

4   Dust with sifted icing sugar and serve straight away with cream and amaretti biscuits.

JUNE

Asparagus, again, should be great now and it's also the time for English strawberries. They are, of course, perfect on their own with fresh cream (which if, like me, you come from the West Country just has to be clotted) but they are also gorgeous served as a topping for my moist and sensuous cheesecake on page 65. Cherries and gooseberries are also coming in. Try slow-cooking them in the same way as the Rhubarb and Orange Compôte on page 22 to serve warm or cold with generous helpings of custard or ice-cream.

Vegetables

Asparagus
Aubergines (eggplants)
Broad (fava) beans
Broccoli (calabrese)
Carrots
Cauliflowers
Courgettes (zucchini)
Cucumbers
Florence fennel
French (green) beans
Globe artichokes
Green garlic
Lettuces
Mangetout (snow peas)
New potatoes
Pea shoots
Peas
Radishes
Rhubarb (outdoor)
Rocket (arugula)
Runner beans (towards
     end of the month)
Sorrel
Spring onions (scallions)
Turnips
Watercress

Fruit and nuts

Avocados (Fuerte, Hass)
Cherries
Elderflowers
Gooseberries
Kiwi fruit
Lychees
Mangoes
Tomatoes
Strawberries

Meat, poultry and game

Lamb
Quail
Venison
Wood pigeon

Fish and seafood

Bream
Brown shrimp
Cod
Crabs
Crayfish
Dover sole
Dublin bay prawns
     (scampi)
Haddock
Halibut
Herring
John Dory
Lemon sole
Lobster
Mackerel
Plaice
Pollack
Prawns
River trout (brown,
     rainbow)
Salmon
Sardines
Sea bass
Sea trout

Produce in *italics* is UK seasonal fare at its peak.

Carrot and coriander is another very popular, classic flavour combination. Adding the ground almonds not only imparts creaminess and an interesting texture but also provides extra nutrients. I have used fragrant ground coriander when cooking the soup, and then blended in chopped fresh coriander leaves at the end for a real burst of flavour.

carrot and almond soup
with coriander

SERVES 4

15 g/½ oz/1 tbsp butter
1 onion, chopped
4 large carrots, sliced
50 g/2 oz/½ cup ground almonds
2.5 ml/½ tsp ground coriander
750 ml/1¼ pt/3 cups boiling chicken
   or vegetable stock

Salt and freshly ground black pepper
30 ml/2 tbsp chopped fresh
   coriander (cilantro), plus a little
   extra to garnish
4 small spoonfuls of crème fraîche

1   Melt the butter in a pan, add the onion and carrots and fry, stirring, for 2 minutes until the onions are softened but not browned. Tip into the crock pot.

2   Add the almonds, ground coriander and stock and season lightly. Cover and cook on High for 3 hours or Low for 6 hours until the carrots are really tender.

3   Purée the soup in a blender or food processor with the chopped coriander. Taste and re-season, if necessary. Return to the crock pot and leave on Low until ready to serve ladled into warm bowls, topped with a small spoonful of crème fraîche and sprinkled with a little chopped coriander.

Boiling artichokes in a pan always gives you a steamy kitchen. Slow-cooking them does away with that. Make sure you add the lemon juice to help retain a little of the colour. To eat the cooked artichokes, pull off a leaf at a time, dip them in the salsa, then pull the fleshy part through the teeth. When all the leaves are eaten, eat the fleshy heart and base with a knife and fork.

globe artichokes with olive and sun-blush tomato salsa

SERVES 4

4 globe artichokes
A good pinch of salt
30 ml/2 tbsp lemon juice

FOR THE SALSA:
12 stoned (pitted) black olives, chopped
12 stoned green olives, chopped
50 g/2 oz sun-blush tomatoes, chopped

10 ml/2 tsp pickled capers, chopped
15 ml/1 tbsp chopped fresh basil
5 ml/1 tsp crushed dried chillies
90 ml/6 tbsp olive oil
Finely grated zest and juice of ½ lime
A good pinch of unrefined caster (superfine) sugar
Freshly ground black pepper

1   Twist off the stalks from the artichokes (the strings will come away with the stalks). Trim the bases, if necessary, so they will stand upright and trim the tips of the leaves with scissors. Stand the artichokes in the crock pot and add enough boiling water to cover them, then add the salt and lemon juice. Cover and cook on High for 2 hours or Low for 4 hours until a leaf pulls away easily.

2   Meanwhile, mix together all the salsa ingredients and chill until ready to serve.

3   When the artichokes are cooked, remove them from the slow cooker, leave to cool, then pull out the small leaves from the centre top. Scoop out the feathery choke underneath with a spoon so you form a well in the middle of each artichoke surrounded by the fat, fleshy-based leaves. Leave until cold, then chill.

4   When ready to serve, stand an artichoke on each of four small plates. Spoon the salsa into the centres and serve.

We are encouraged to eat more heart-healthy oily fish, and fresh sardines are superb. They are often grilled but it's very easy to overcook them, in which case they can take on an unpleasantly bitter taste. Gentle slow-cooking renders them moist, succulent and sweet and the herbs, garlic and lemon bring out their full flavour.

sardines with herbs, garlic and lemon

SERVES 4

8–12 sardines (depending on size),
  cleaned and scaled
60 ml/4 tbsp chopped fresh parsley
30 ml/2 tbsp chopped fresh thyme
2 garlic cloves, finely chopped
Finely grated zest and juice of
  ½ lemon

Salt and freshly ground black pepper
60 ml/4 tbsp boiling water

TO SERVE:
Crusty bread

1 Rinse the fish inside and out and pat dry with kitchen paper (paper towel). Lay the fish in the crock pot. Sprinkle with half the parsley, the thyme, garlic, lemon zest and juice and some salt and pepper.

2 Spoon the boiling water over the sardines, cover and cook on Low for 1 hour.

3 Carefully lift the fish out of the crock pot and arrange on serving plates. Sprinkle with the remaining parsley and serve with crusty bread.

This is a modern version of the Greek speciality moussaka, and you could use two aubergines, sliced lengthways, instead of the courgettes if you prefer. I would suggest, though, that you either blanch them in boiling water for 2 minutes and drain well or cook the strips on an oiled griddle pan for 2 minutes on each side before layering.

steak and courgette layer with feta and olives

SERVES 4

15 ml/1 tbsp olive oil, plus extra for greasing
1 onion, chopped
450 g/1 lb lean minced (ground) steak
1 large garlic clove, crushed
5 ml/1 tsp ground cinnamon
5 ml/1 tsp dried oregano
30 ml/2 tbsp tomato purée (paste)
30 ml/2 tbsp red wine
5 ml/1 tsp unrefined caster (superfine) sugar

Salt and freshly ground black pepper
5–6 small courgettes (zucchini)
100 g/4 oz/1 cup crumbled Feta cheese
120 ml/4 fl oz/½ cup crème fraîche
30 ml/2 tbsp chopped fresh parsley
8–12 stoned (pitted) black olives, halved

TO SERVE:
Pitta breads and a mixed salad

1 Heat the oil in a saucepan, add the onion, steak and garlic and fry, stirring, until the meat is no longer pink and all the grains are separate.

2 Stir in the cinnamon, oregano, tomato purée, wine and sugar, cover and simmer, stirring occasionally for 5 minutes. Season to taste.

3 Trim the courgettes and cut lengthways into fairly thin slices.

4 Oil a shallow rectangular dish that will sit in the crock pot. Put a layer of courgettes in the base, add half the meat, then top with half the remaining courgettes. Repeat the layers, ending with courgettes.

5 Mix the cheese with the crème fraîche, parsley and some pepper and spread over the courgettes; the courgettes should still show a little through the sauce. Sprinkle the olives over.

6   Place in the crock pot with enough boiling water to come half-way up the side of the dish. Cover and cook on High for 2–3 hours or Low for 4–6 hours until the courgettes are tender.

7   Serve hot with pitta breads and a mixed salad.

Barley has become one of my favourite grains. Rice can overcook and become soggy if you aren't careful, but barley behaves perfectly in the slow cooker. It retains its nutty texture and the grains stay separate even when creamy. Here I've used Blue Vinney cheese, a speciality from Dorset, but you could use any well-flavoured cheese for this dish.

broad bean and blue vinney barley risotto

SERVES 4–6

30 ml/2 tbsp olive oil
1 onion, chopped
1 garlic clove, crushed
450 g/1 lb baby broad (fava) beans, shelled (about 225 g/8 oz shelled weight)
350 g/12 oz/generous 1⅔ cups pearl barley
900 ml/1½ pts/3¾ cups boiling vegetable stock

Salt and freshly ground black pepper
30 ml/2 tbsp chopped fresh sage
100 g/4 oz Blue Vinney cheese, cut into small dice
90 ml/6 tbsp single (light) cream
15 ml/1 tbsp chopped fresh parsley

TO SERVE:
Ciabatta bread and an avocado and pea shoot salad

1   Heat the oil in a frying pan. Add the onion and garlic and fry, stirring, for 2 minutes until softened but not browned. Stir in the broad beans and barley until glistening, then tip into the crock pot.

2   Add the stock, some salt and pepper and half the sage. Stir well, cover and cook on High for 2 hours or Low for 4 hours until the barley and broad beans are tender.

3   Turn off the slow cooker. Gently stir in the cheese, cream and parsley. Cover and leave for 5 minutes.

4   Spoon into warm bowls and sprinkle with the remaining sage. Serve with ciabatta bread and an avocado and pea shoot salad.

This is something of an indulgence – racks of lamb are not the lowest-priced cuts of the animal, but they are well worth having as a treat! The meat will be tender however cooked, but in the slow-cooker it will become meltingly marvellous. You could cook a small shoulder of lamb, chopped into quarters, in the same way as a cheaper alternative.

racks of lamb with baby broad beans, turnips and harissa

SERVES 4

4 small racks of lamb with
  3 or 4 cutlets each
15 ml/1 tbsp harissa paste
15 g/½ oz/1 tbsp butter
1 bunch of spring onions (scallions),
  chopped
4 turnips, diced
450 g/1 lb baby broad (fava) beans,
  shelled (about 225 g/8 oz shelled
  weight)

250 ml/8 fl oz/1 cup lamb or
  chicken stock
10 ml/2 tsp tomato purée (paste)
15 ml/1 tbsp chopped fresh thyme
Salt and freshly ground black pepper
Sprigs of fresh thyme to garnish

TO SERVE:
New potatoes

1 If the racks are not already prepared, scrape the meat and fat from about 2.5 cm/1 in from the ends of the bones of the cutlets. Score the fat side of the racks in a criss-cross pattern and rub all over with the harissa paste.

2 Melt the butter in a frying pan, add the lamb and brown quickly all over.

3 Put the spring onions, turnips and beans in the crock pot and lay the lamb on top.

4 Pour the stock into the frying pan and add the tomato purée. Bring to the boil, stirring, then add the thyme and seasoning to taste. Pour over the lamb. Cover and cook on High for 2–3 hours or Low for 4–6 hours until everything is tender.

5 Taste and re-season. if necessary. Serve in warm open soups plates, garnished with sprigs of thyme, with new potatoes handed separately.

Rich cheesecakes are often baked in a very slow oven and, while the results are usually delicious, a cheesecake from a slow cooker will be moister, softer and beautifully pale. When topped with sweet strawberries bathed in a sticky redcurrant glaze, it becomes a spectacular party dessert. I use low-fat soft cheese but the choice is yours.

fresh strawberry cheesecake

SERVES 8–10

200 g/7 oz/1 small packet of chocolate digestive biscuits
75 g/3 oz/⅓ cup butter, plus a little extra for greasing
700 g/1½ lb/3 cups white soft cheese
225 g/8 oz/1 cup unrefined caster (superfine) sugar
2 eggs

5 ml/1 tsp vanilla essence (extract)

FOR THE TOPPING:
60 ml/4 tbsp redcurrant jelly (clear conserve)
15 ml/1 tbsp water
175 g/6 oz strawberries, sliced

TO SERVE:
Crème fraîche

1 Finely crush the biscuits in a plastic bag with a rolling pin. Melt the butter in a saucepan or in a bowl in the microwave and stir in the biscuit crumbs. Grease a 20 cm/8 in springform cake tin.

2 Place the tin in a sheet of foil and press it up the sides of the tin (to prevent water seeping in). Press the crumb mixture into the base and a little way up the side of the prepared tin.

3 Beat the cheese with the sugar, eggs and vanilla essence. Spoon into the tin. Cover the tin with foil, twisting and folding under the rim to secure, and place in the crock pot. Pour in enough boiling water to cover the base of the crock pot. Cover and cook on Low for 3–4 hours until just firm.

4 Remove the tin from the crock pot and allow the cheesecake to cool, then chill.

5 To make the topping, heat the redcurrant jelly with the water in a saucepan, stirring, until melted. Transfer the cheesecake to a serving plate. Brush a little of the glaze over the top of the cheesecake, then arrange the strawberries attractively over the surface. Brush the remaining glaze all over the strawberries so they are all coated. Leave to set, then serve with crème fraîche.

These moist, chocolaty morsels are so moreish that you'll find it difficult to stick to having just one. When cherries aren't in season, experiment with fresh blueberries or dried fruits such as raisins or cranberries. Chopped walnuts can also be added for loads of delicious variations. If using dried fruit or nuts, add 15 ml/1 tbsp of water to the mixture.

black forest brownies

MAKES 15

50 g/2 oz/¼ cup butter, plus extra for greasing
100 g/4 oz/½ cup unrefined caster (superfine) sugar
75 g/3 oz plain (semi-sweet) chocolate with at least 70 per cent cocoa solids
75 g/3 oz/¾ cup self-raising flour
15 ml/1 tbsp cocoa (unsweetened chocolate) powder

A pinch of salt
2.5 ml/½ tsp vanilla essence (extract)
2 eggs, beaten
175 g/6 oz cherries, halved and stoned (pitted)
30 ml/2 tbsp icing (confectioners') sugar, sifted

1   Grease a shallow rectangular dish measuring about 18 × 23 cm/ 7 × 9 in that will fit in a large crock pot.

2   Melt the butter, sugar and chocolate in a pan over a gentle heat, stirring occasionally.

3   Sift together the flour, cocoa and salt in a bowl. Stir in the melted mixture, the vanilla essence and eggs and beat well. Fold in the cherries.

4   Turn the mixture into the prepared dish. Cover loosely with foil, twisting and folding under the rim to secure. Place in the crock pot and pour in enough boiling water to come half-way up the sides of the dish. Cover and cook on High for 1½ hours until firm to the touch.

5   Remove the dish from the crock pot and leave to cool.

6   Dust with the icing sugar, then cut into squares and remove from the dish. Store in an airtight container.

JULY

Now you'll have an abundance of fabulous home-grown fruit and vegetables to drool over. You'll find everything from aubergines to zucchini (okay, I know that's not the British name for courgettes – but you know what I mean!) and sumptuous soft fruits like raspberries, blueberries, all the fresh currants and, of course, lovely fragrant home-grown tomatoes of all shapes and sizes. Many of these seasonal delights benefit from slow-cooking and many more make perfect accompaniments to summer dishes.

Vegetables
Aubergines (eggplants)
Beetroot (red beets)
Broad (fava) beans
Broccoli (calabrese)
Carrots
Cauliflowers
Courgettes (zucchini)
Cucumbers
Florence fennel
French (green) beans
Garlic
Globe artichokes
Kohl rabi
Lettuces
Mangetout (snow peas)
New potatoes
Onions
Peas
(Bell) peppers
Potatoes (old, maincrop)
Radishes
Rocket (arugula)
Runner beans
Samphire
Sorrel
Sweetcorn
Swiss chard
Turnips
Watercress

Fruit and nuts
Apricots
Avocados (Fuerte, Hass)
Bilberries/wortleberries
Blackberries
Blackcurrants
Blueberries
Gooseberries
Greengages
Kiwi fruit
Loganberries
Lychees
Mangoes
Melons
Nectarines
Peaches
Raspberries
Redcurrants
Strawberries
Tomatoes
Whitecurrants

Meat, poultry and game
Lamb
Quail
Rabbit
Veal (English)
Venison
Wood pigeon

Fish and seafood
Bream
Brown shrimp
Cod
Crabs
Crayfish
Dover sole
*Dublin bay prawns
    (scampi)*
Haddock
Herring
John Dory
Lemon sole
Lobster
Mackerel
Plaice
Pollack
Prawns
River trout (brown,
    rainbow)
Salmon
Sardines
Scallops
Sea bass
Sea trout

Produce in *italics* is UK seasonal fare at its peak.

This is a very simple soup that tastes really good both hot and chilled. You can vary the vegetables you use with the beetroot, depending on what is in season – parsnip or swede for instance. Try a couple of grated celery sticks instead of the turnip, too. You could use crème fraîche or thick yoghurt instead of soured cream to spoon on top, if you prefer.

beetroot, carrot and turnip soup

SERVES 4

2 large beetroot (red beets), coarsely grated
2 carrots, coarsely grated
1 large turnip, coarsely grated
1 onion, grated
750 ml/1¼ pts/3 cups boiling chicken or vegetable stock

15 ml/1 tbsp red wine vinegar
Salt and freshly ground black pepper
30 ml/2 tbsp soured (dairy sour) cream
15 ml/1 tbsp chopped fresh dill (dill weed)

1 Put the grated vegetables in the crock pot and pour the boiling stock over. Cover and cook on High for 2 hours or Low for 4 hours.

2 Stir in the vinegar and season to taste. Ladle into warm bowls, add a swirl of soured cream to each and sprinkle with the dill.

This is the soup to make when you have a glut of home-grown tomatoes.
You can omit the vodka, if you prefer, but it does provide a fabulous kick!
You could use an ordinary chopped onion but you would need to soften it
in 15 ml/1 tbsp of olive oil before adding to the crock pot or the flavour
would be too harsh.

fresh tomato and basil soup
with vodka

SERVES 6

900 g/2 lb ripe tomatoes, skinned
   and chopped
1 bunch of spring onions (scallions),
   chopped
10 ml/2 tsp unrefined caster
   (superfine) sugar
15 ml/1 tbsp tomato purée (paste)
15 ml/1 tbsp white balsamic
   condiment

45 ml/3 tbsp olive oil
300 ml/½ pt/1¼ cups boiling chicken
   or vegetable stock
2 thick slices of ciabatta bread,
   made into breadcrumbs
30 ml/2 tbsp chopped fresh basil
Salt and freshly ground black pepper
30–45 ml/2–3 tbsp vodka
6 tiny sprigs of basil to garnish

1   Put the tomatoes in the crock pot with the spring onions, sugar,
    tomato purée, balsamic condiment, oil and stock. Cover and
    cook on High for 2 hours or Low for 4 hours until the tomatoes
    are pulpy.

2   Stir in the breadcrumbs and basil and season well. Cover and cook
    on High for a further 30 minutes or on Low for 1 hour.

3   Stir in the vodka. Ladle into warm bowls and garnish each serving
    with a tiny sprig of fresh basil.

This is equally delicious made with herrings. Make sure you remove as many bones as possible before rolling for maximum pleasure when eating! White balsamic condiment is like a vinegar, and will be found among them on the supermarket shelves, but it doesn't contain enough acid for it to be officially classified as one. You can use wine vinegar instead for a sharper flavour.

pickled rolled mackerel
with fennel and onion

SERVES 4

4 small mackerel, cleaned, heads
   and tails removed
Salt and freshly ground black pepper
1 small onion, halved and thinly
   sliced
1 head of fennel, thinly shredded
250 ml/8 fl oz/1 cup white balsamic
   condiment
250 ml/8 fl oz/1 cup water

15 ml/1 tbsp unrefined caster
   (superfine) sugar
2 bay leaves

TO SERVE:
Multigrain bread spread with
   unsalted (sweet) butter and a
   green salad

1   Slit each fish down to the tail and open up. Lay the fish one at a time on a board, skin-side up. Run your thumb firmly down the centre of the fish, from the head end to the tail, several times. Turn the fish over and carefully remove the backbone and any loose bones and trim off the fins. Cut each fillet in half lengthways.

2   Sprinkle with salt and pepper, add a few of the onion slices and a little of the shredded fennel to each and roll up from the head end.

3   Place the fish in the crock pot, tail-sides down, and scatter the rest of the fennel over.

4   Put the balsamic condiment, water and sugar in a saucepan and bring to the boil. Stir to dissolve the sugar, then pour over the fish. Add the bay leaves. Cover and cook on Low for 1–2 hours until cooked through.

5   Transfer the rolls to a container with a sealable lid and pour the cooking liquid over. Leave to cool, then cover and chill.

6   Drain well and serve cold with multigrain bread spread with unsalted butter and a green salad.

The fresh redcurrants in this recipe add a touch of tartness that offsets the richness of the meat. You can use sweet sherry or Madeira if you prefer instead of port, which would add a slightly different, nuttier flavour. You can also make this recipe substituting lamb shanks or a small lamb shoulder chopped into quarters for the pork chops (and use lamb stock too).

slow-roast pork chops in port with redcurrants

SERVES 4

Salt and freshly ground black pepper
4 thick pork chops, about 175 g/
    6 oz each
15 g/½ oz/1 tbsp butter
15 ml/1 tbsp sunflower oil
15 ml/1 tbsp chopped fresh
    rosemary
1 onion, finely chopped
200 ml/7 fl oz/scant 1 cup beef or
    pork stock

45 ml/3 tbsp port
30 ml/2 tbsp redcurrant jelly (clear
    conserve)
175 g/6 oz fresh redcurrants
4 small sprigs of fresh rosemary to
    garnish

TO SERVE:
New potatoes and mangetout (snow
    peas)

1   Season the chops. Heat the butter and oil in a frying pan, add the chops and brown quickly. Remove from the pan with a draining spoon and place in the crock pot. Sprinkle with the chopped rosemary.

2   Add the onion to the frying pan and fry, stirring, for 2 minutes. Pour the stock, port and redcurrant jelly into the pan and bring to the boil, stirring to melt the jelly. Season, then pour over the meat. Cover and cook on High for 3 hours or Low for 6 hours until meltingly tender.

3   Carefully lift out the chops and keep warm. Reserve 4 small sprigs of redcurrants for garnish and remove the rest from their stalks with the prongs of a fork.

4   Spoon off any excess fat from the crock pot, then pour the juices into a small saucepan. Bring to the boil, throw in the redcurrants and boil for 3–4 minutes until the sauce is reduced and slightly thickened. Taste and re-season, if necessary.

5   Transfer the chops to warm serving plates and spoon the redcurrant juices over. Garnish each chop with a small sprig of redcurrants and a sprig of rosemary. Serve hot with new potatoes and mangetout.

British veal is excellent now and is not inhumanely reared, as it is on some parts of the Continent. In this recipe slices are rolled with smoked cured ham, fresh sage and Cheddar cheese, then gently braised. Use outdoor-reared pork or beaten out chicken breasts instead of veal, if you prefer. You could serve the vegetable braise as a soup, sprinkled with freshly grated Parmesan cheese.

veal rolls with smoked ham and cheese

SERVES 4

4 veal escalopes
4 thin slices of oak-smoked ham
50 g/2 oz/½ cup grated Cheddar cheese
50 g/2 oz/1 cup fresh breadcrumbs
15 ml/1 tbsp chopped fresh sage
Salt and freshly ground black pepper
1 egg, beaten
15 g/½ oz/1 tbsp butter
15 ml/1 tbsp olive oil
1 onion, very finely chopped

1 carrot, very finely chopped
1 head of fennel, very finely chopped
750 ml/1¼ pts/3 cups boiling chicken or vegetable stock
1 bouquet garni sachet
30 ml/2 tbsp chopped fresh parsley, plus extra to garnish

TO SERVE:
Sauté potatoes, green beans and a tomato salad

1 Put the veal escalopes one at a time in a plastic bag and beat with a rolling pin or meat mallet to flatten. Lay a slice of ham on each.

2 Mix the cheese with the breadcrumbs, sage and some salt and pepper. Mix with the egg to bind. Spread over the ham, then roll up each escalope and secure with cocktail sticks (toothpicks).

3 Melt the butter and oil in a large frying pan. Add the veal and brown quickly all over. Remove from the pan with a draining spoon and set aside.

4 Add the prepared vegetables to the pan and fry, stirring, for 2 minutes. Transfer to the crock pot.

5 Arrange the veal on top of the vegetables. Add the stock and bouquet garni, cover and cook on High for 2 hours or Low for 4 hours.

6   Turn off the slow cooker and leave the veal in the pot to keep warm. Spoon about 150 ml/¼ pt/⅔ cup of the cooking liquid into a saucepan and boil rapidly for several minutes until reduced by half and syrupy. Taste and re-season if necessary. Add the parsley.

7   Carefully lift the veal out of the crock pot. Remove the cocktail sticks and slice thickly. Arrange the slices on serving plates and spoon a little of the reduced cooking juices over. Serve hot, garnished with parsley, with sauté potatoes, green beans and a tomato salad.

I find stuffed vegetables naturally lend themselves to eastern Mediterranean flavours such as oregano, cinnamon, olives and Feta cheese – my Cabbage Leaves Stuffed with Swede, Bulghar and Pine Nuts on page 28 are witness to this! Instead of couscous, you could use 100 g/ 4 oz of minced lamb, browned first in just a little olive oil, if you prefer.

stuffed aubergines with tomatoes and couscous

SERVES 4

2 aubergines (eggplants), halved lengthways
60 ml/4 tbsp olive oil
50 g/2 oz/⅓ cup couscous
120 ml/4 fl oz/½ cup boiling water
2 large ripe tomatoes, skinned and diced
2 large garlic cloves, crushed
2.5 ml/½ tsp ground cinnamon
5 ml/1 tsp dried oregano

12 stoned (pitted) black olives, halved
Salt and freshly ground black pepper
100 g/4 oz/1 cup crumbled Feta cheese
30 ml/2 tbsp chopped fresh parsley to garnish

TO SERVE:
Warm pitta bread and a green salad

1   Gently scoop out the aubergine flesh with a teaspoon, following the natural contour of the seeded area to leave a border about 5 mm/¼ in all round. Finely chop the scooped-out flesh.

2   Heat the oil in a frying pan, add the aubergine flesh and fry gently, stirring, for about 3 minutes until softened and turning brown in places. Remove from the heat.

3   Put the couscous in a bowl and add the boiling water. Stir, then leave to stand for 5 minutes to absorb the water. Fluff up with a fork, then mix with the aubergine flesh, the tomatoes, garlic, cinnamon, oregano and olives. Season to taste. Pile the mixture back in the aubergine shells.

4   Place the aubergine shells in the crock pot and pour in just enough boiling water to cover the base. Scatter the cheese over each aubergine half. Cover and cook on High for 2 hours or Low for 4 hours until the aubergine shells are really tender.

5 Carefully lift the aubergines out of the crock pot with a fish slice and transfer to serving plates. Garnish with the parsley and serve with warm pitta bread and a green salad.

This is fabulous served as a light lunch with lots of crusty bread but it's also a great accompaniment to grilled meats – particularly as a side dish for a barbecue party. The saltiness of the Halloumi complements the sweetness of the peas and kohl rabi. You could use turnips or radishes instead of kohl rabi.

kohl rabi with garlic, peas and halloumi cheese

SERVES 4–6

2 large kohl rabi, peeled and diced
2 garlic cloves, crushed
225 g/8 oz/2 cups shelled fresh
   peas
90 ml/6 tbsp boiling chicken or
   vegetable stock
Salt and freshly ground black pepper
A good knob of butter, cut into small
   flakes

30 ml/2 tbsp chopped fresh mint
250 g/9 oz block of Halloumi
   cheese, diced

TO SERVE:
Crusty bread

1 Put the kohl rabi, garlic, peas and stock in the crock pot with a little salt and pepper. Cover and cook on High for 2 hours or Low for 4 hours until tender.

2 Stir in the butter flakes, most of the mint and the cheese. Cover and leave on Low for 10–15 minutes until the cheese softens.

3 Serve in bowls, sprinkled with the remaining mint and lots of crusty bread.

You could use another white soft cheese – even supermarket own brands – if you like. I just prefer the texture and flavour of ricotta. You can also use nectarines, which will also be at their best right now, instead of peaches or, when in season, try English plums or greengages, though you will need twice as many, of course, as they are much smaller.

hot stuffed peaches with ricotta, almonds and candied ginger

SERVES 4

4 small just-ripe peaches
100 g/4 oz/½ cup ricotta cheese
30 ml/2 tbsp chopped candied
  ginger

50 g/2 oz/½ cup ground almonds
50 g/2 oz/¼ cup unrefined caster
  (superfine) sugar
90 ml/6 tbsp boiling water

1   Halve the peaches and remove the stones (pits). Cut a very thin slice off the rounded side of each half so it will stand firmly. Chop the cut-off slices.

2   Mix the cheese with the ginger, almonds, 15 ml/1 tbsp of the sugar and the chopped peach slices.

3   Stand the peaches in the crock pot and spoon the filling into each. Mix the remaining sugar with the boiling water and pour around the peaches. Cover and cook on Low for 2 hours.

4   Serve hot with the syrup spooned around.

This dessert is an ingenious way of making a fruit fool without all the stirring that is essential when you cook one conventionally. This custard cooks so slowly it doesn't form lumps and the whole thing is simply served straight from the individual dishes. Try it with other soft fruits or berries, such as strawberries, raspberries and blackcurrants, too.

hot whole fruit blueberry fool

SERVES 4

30 ml/2 tbsp cornflour (cornstarch)
200 ml/7 fl oz/scant 1 cup milk
1 egg
60 ml/4 tbsp unrefined caster
  (superfine) sugar
5 ml/1 tsp vanilla essence (extract)

200 ml/7 fl oz/scant 1 cup single
  (light) cream
100 g/4 oz ripe blueberries

TO SERVE:
Shortbread

1 Blend the cornflour with 60 ml/4 tbsp of the milk in a bowl. Whisk in the egg, sugar and vanilla.

2 Pour the remaining milk and the cream into a pan. Bring almost to the boil, then pour into the cornflour mixture, whisking all the time.

3 Reserve a few blueberries for decoration and divide the remainder between four ramekins (custard cups). Pour the custard over.

4 Stand the dishes in the crock pot and pour round enough boiling water to come half-way up the sides. Cover and cook on Low for 2 hours until set.

5 Decorate with the reserved blueberries and serve with shortbread.

AUGUST

This is a wonderful time of year for home-grown produce. Beans, peas, salad vegetables, sweetcorn, peppers, melons and berries of all colours, shapes and sizes are around. You should also enjoy the soft fruits from further afield — and it's the season for perfect peaches and nectarines too. There's plenty of seafood and, on the twelfth of the month, the grouse season starts in England.

Vegetables
Aubergines (eggplants)
Beetroot (red beets)
Broad (fava) beans
Broccoli (calabrese)
Carrots
Cavolo nero (black cabbage)
Chillies
Courgettes (zucchini)
Cucumbers
Florence fennel
French (green) beans
Garlic
Globe artichokes
Kohl rabi
Lettuces
Mangetout (snow peas)
Onions
Peas
(Bell) peppers
Potatoes (old, maincrop)
Radishes
Rocket (arugula)
Runner beans
Samphire
Sorrel
Sweetcorn
Swiss chard
Watercress

Fruit and nuts
Apricots
Avocados (Hass)
Blackberries
Blackcurrants
Blueberries
Greengages
Loganberries
Mangoes
Melons
Nectarines
Papaya (paw paw)
Peaches
Plums
Raspberries
Redcurrants
Tayberries
Tomatoes
Whitecurrants

Meat, poultry and game
Grouse
Lamb
Quail
Rabbit
Venison
Wood pigeon

Fish and seafood
Bream
Brown shrimp
Cod
Crabs
Crayfish
Dublin bay prawns (scampi)
Dover sole
Grey mullet
Haddock
Halibut
Herring
John Dory
Lemon sole
Lobster
Mackerel
Monkfish
Plaice
Pollack
Red mullet
River trout (brown, rainbow)
Salmon
Sardines
Scallops
Sea bass
Squid
Whitebait

Produce in *italics* is UK seasonal fare at its peak.

What better way to celebrate all the lovely vegetables around now but in a Mediterranean-style soup with loads of colour, texture and flavour? It simply begs to have freshly grated Parmesan cheese sprinkled over and I particularly like to serve warm olive ciabatta with it. And it really couldn't be simpler; all the ingredients just go in the crock pot at the beginning.

summer
vegetable soup

SERVES 6

1 onion, finely chopped
1 carrot, finely chopped
1 red (bell) pepper, finely chopped
1 yellow pepper, finely chopped
2 courgettes (zucchini), finely
   chopped
50 g/2 oz French (green) beans,
   cut into small pieces
1 garlic clove, crushed
100 g/4 oz/1 cup shelled fresh peas
450 g/1 lb ripe tomatoes, skinned
   and chopped

750 ml/1¼ pts/3 cups boiling
   chicken or vegetables stock
30 ml/2 tbsp chopped fresh oregano
5 ml/1 tsp unrefined caster
   (superfine) sugar
Salt and freshly ground black pepper

TO SERVE:
Freshly grated Parmesan cheese

1   Put all the ingredients in the crock pot. Cover and cook on High for 3 hours or Low for 6 hours until everything is tender.

2   Stir well, taste and re-season, if necessary. Ladle into warm bowls and serve with freshly grated Parmesan cheese.

Because of its firm texture and definable taste, sea bass lends itself to the sweet spicy flavours of Chinese and other Asian cuisines. It's another of my favourite fish as its flavour is just exquisite, but you could use bream or even river trout in the recipe. You could also use four small fish instead of one large one as the flesh won't break up during the slow cooking.

whole sea bass in soy and ginger marinade with vegetables and noodles

SERVES 4

5 ml/1 tsp grated fresh root ginger
1 garlic clove, crushed
15 ml/1 tbsp soy sauce
15 ml/1 tbsp dry sherry
10 ml/2 tsp clear honey
15 ml/1 tbsp lemon juice
1 sea bass, about 1 kg/2¼ lb, cleaned
15 ml/1 tbsp sunflower oil
5 ml/1 tsp sesame oil
3 carrots, thinly sliced

2 courgettes (zucchini), cut into matchsticks
1 red (bell) pepper, cut into thin strips
1 onion, halved and thinly sliced
225 g/8 oz/1 small can of bamboo shoots, drained
150 ml/¼ pt/⅔ cup boiling chicken or fish stock
300 g/11 oz fresh egg noodles

1 Mix the ginger with the garlic, soy sauce, sherry, honey and lemon juice in a shallow dish, large enough to take the fish.

2 Make several slashes in the flesh of the fish on both sides. Add to the marinade, turn it over and leave to marinate for 2 hours, turning occasionally.

3 Heat the oils in a frying pan. Add the prepared vegetables and the bamboo shoots and fry, stirring, for 2 minutes. Transfer to the crock pot and lay the fish on top. Tip any marinade over and add the boiling stock. Cover and cook on Low for 2–3 hours.

4 Carefully lift the fish out of the pot and keep warm. Pour the cooking liquid into a saucepan and boil rapidly to reduce slightly.

5 Meanwhile, add the noodles to the vegetables in the crock pot, toss, cover and leave in the crock pot, still on Low.

6 Fillet the fish and cut it into four pieces. To serve, pile the vegetables and noodles on to four warm plates, top with the fish and spoon the reduced cooking juices over.

This is very easy to prepare. You simply blend all the ingredients for the custards, then pop them in the slow cooker to set. They can be eaten straight away, but could also be kept chilled in the fridge for up to 3 days, covered securely in clingfilm to prevent them drying out. You won't need to add much salt as smoked salmon is already quite salty.

salmon custards
with rocket

SERVES 6

225 g/8 oz salmon fillet, skinned
  and cut into chunks
100 g/4 oz smoked salmon
  trimmings
30 ml/2 tbsp chopped fresh parsley
150 ml/¼ pt/⅔ cup mayonnaise
150 ml/¼ pt/⅔ cup single (light)
  cream
2 eggs
5 ml/1 tsp lemon juice

Salt and freshly ground black pepper
A little sunflower oil for greasing
4 thin slices of cucumber
6 small handfuls of rocket (arugula)
30 ml/2 tbsp olive oil
15 ml/1 tbsp balsamic vinegar

TO SERVE:
Multigrain rolls

1 With the motor of a blender or food processor running, drop in the fresh and smoked salmon, then the parsley, mayonnaise, cream, eggs, lemon juice and salt and pepper to taste.

2 Lightly oil six ramekins (custard cups). Tip the salmon mixture into them and place in the crock pot (you may need to rest one of the dishes on the rims of the others). Pour round 2.5 cm/1 in of boiling water, cover and cook on Low for 2 hours until set.

3 Remove from the crock pot and leave to cool, then chill.

4 When ready to serve, loosen slightly and turn out on to small plates. Arrange a twist of cucumber on top of each. Put a small pile of rocket leaves to one side and drizzle the olive oil and balsamic vinegar over the rocket and around the edge of the plate. Add a good grinding of pepper. Serve with multigrain rolls.

Store the oil in a suitable container and use it for cooking other meat or for sautéing potatoes. If not eaten straight away, the rabbit can be stored in its oil for several days in the fridge (make sure it is completely submerged and in a sealed container), then drained and sautéed in a non-stick frying pan before serving. Chicken or duck can also be cooked this way.

rabbit and
garlic confit

SERVES 4

5 ml/1 tsp coarse sea salt
5 ml/1 tsp dried thyme
A good pinch of ground cloves
1 rabbit, cut into 4–6 portions
1 head of garlic, separated into
  cloves and peeled
2 bay leaves

450 ml/¾ pt/2 cups olive oil
450 ml/¾ pt/2 cups sunflower oil

TO SERVE:
Very fresh French bread, cold
  unsalted (sweet) butter and a
  crisp green salad

1 Mix the salt with the thyme and cloves. Rub the rabbit all over with the mixture and leave to stand for at least 2 hours.

2 Pat the rabbit dry on kitchen paper (paper towels) and place in the crock pot. Add all the garlic cloves and the bay leaves.

3 Heat the oils until almost boiling (when tiny bubbles are beginning to rise to the surface) and pour over the rabbit (it will sizzle slightly). Cover and cook on Low for 4 hours.

4 Lift the rabbit out of the oil, drain on kitchen paper, then transfer to warm plates. Drain the garlic cloves, and divide between the plates. To serve, mash the garlic with cold unsalted butter and spread on slices of fresh French bread to eat with the rabbit and a crisp green salad.

Peas and lamb have long been good companions and this is a lovely way to serve them together. Mint is another firm favourite with this delicious meat and it's used to flavour it before cooking. You may find the lamb falls apart when you cut it but this doesn't matter – it will still taste delicious! Redcurrant jelly is the obvious condiment to accompany the dish.

slow-roast leg of lamb with mint and fresh peas

SERVES 4–6

½ lean leg of lamb, about 1 kg/2¼ lb, trimmed of excess fat
1 large garlic clove, cut into thin slivers
60 ml/4 tbsp chopped fresh mint
450 g/1 lb small potatoes, scrubbed
Salt and freshly ground black pepper
250 ml/8 fl oz/1 cup boiling lamb stock

225 g/8 oz/2 cups shelled fresh peas
45 ml/3 tbsp cornflour (cornstarch)
45 ml/3 tbsp water

TO SERVE:
Carrots and redcurrant jelly (clear conserve)

1 Make small slits all over the lamb with the point of a knife and insert a sliver of garlic into each. Lay the meat in the crock pot and sprinkle with half the mint.

2 Put the potatoes all round and season everything with salt and pepper. Pour the boiling stock around, cover and cook on Low for 7 hours until everything is really tender.

3 Add the peas and cook for a further 1 hour.

4 Transfer the lamb to a carving dish and keep warm. Lift out the peas and potatoes with a draining spoon and place in a dish. Keep warm.

5 Spoon off any fat from the juices. Blend the cornflour with the water in a small saucepan. Add the cooking liquor, bring to the boil and cook for 1 minute, stirring, until slightly thickened. Season to taste.

6 Cut the lamb into pieces and place on warm plates with the potatoes and peas. Spoon the gravy over the lamb and sprinkle with the remaining mint. Serve with carrots and redcurrant jelly.

This is so simple to prepare but it is packed with flavour and, of course, has a wonderful vibrant red colour. I like it with ribbon noodles, such as tagliatelle or papardelle, but you can serve it with rice or fluffy mashed potatoes if you prefer. The dish has all the flavours of Spanish cuisine – in fact Spanish paprika is another name for pimènton.

red pepper chicken
with chorizo

SERVES 4

30 ml/2 tbsp olive oil
1 onion, chopped
1 garlic clove, crushed
2 red (bell) peppers, sliced
1 or 2 fat red chillies, seeded and sliced
50 g/2 oz piece of chorizo, skinned and sliced
4 skinless chicken breasts
400 g/14 oz/1 large can of chopped tomatoes
60 ml/4 tbsp dry white wine

15 ml/1 tbsp tomato purée (paste)
30 ml/2 tbsp cornflour (cornstarch)
30 ml/2 tbsp water
5 ml/1 tsp unrefined caster (superfine) sugar
2.5 ml/½ tsp dried oregano
2.5 ml/½ tsp pimènton (smoked paprika)
Salt and freshly ground black pepper

TO SERVE:
Ribbon noodles and a crisp green salad

1   Heat the oil in a saucepan, add the onion, garlic, peppers and chillies and fry, stirring, for 2 minutes until softened and just beginning to colour slightly. Tip into the crock pot. Add the chorizo and chicken.

2   Put the tomatoes, wine and tomato purée in the saucepan. Blend the cornflour with the water and stir in. Bring to the boil, stirring, then stir in the sugar, oregano, pimènton and salt and pepper to taste. Pour over the chicken. Cover and cook on High for 2–3 hours or Low for 4–6 hours until tender.

3   Serve spooned over ribbon noodles with a crisp green salad.

This wonderfully colourful dish is gorgeous when served with any barbecued, grilled or roasted meats, chicken or fish. It also makes a lovely simple starter with some crusty bread, or you could chill the peppers to serve cold as a salad, if you prefer. Add a finely chopped fat red or green chilli with the garlic, if you would like to introduce a little heat.

pot-roasted rainbow peppers with onions, rosemary and garlic

SERVES 4–6

2 red (bell) peppers, cut into 6 pieces
2 green peppers, cut into 6 pieces
2 yellow peppers, cut into 6 pieces
2 orange peppers, cut into 6 pieces
2 red onions, cut into wedges

2 garlic cloves, finely chopped
1 large sprig of fresh rosemary
75 ml/5 tbsp olive oil
Freshly ground black pepper
Coarse sea salt

1 Spread out the peppers and onions in the crock pot. Scatter the garlic over.

2 Strip the rosemary leaves off their stalks and chop finely. Scatter over the peppers and onions.

3 Trickle the oil all over and add a good grinding of pepper. Cover and cook on High for 1–2 hours or Low for 2–4 hours until tender, stirring quickly once half-way through cooking.

4 Tip the peppers and onions with all the lovely flavoured oil into a serving dish and sprinkle with a few grains of coarse sea salt before serving.

Rice pudding is perfect when cooked in the slow cooker – the result is always creamy, soft and tender. You could substitute the same weight of strawberries for the raspberries in the coulis, but you may need to vary the amount of icing sugar you use, depending on the ripeness of the berries. The lemon or lime juice brings out the full flavour of the fruit.

vanilla rice pudding
with fresh raspberry coulis

SERVES 4

75 g/3 oz/⅓ cup short-grain (pudding) rice
50 g/2 oz/¼ cup unrefined caster (superfine) sugar
1 vanilla pod
410 g/14½ oz/1 large can of evaporated milk

FOR THE COULIS:
100 g/4 oz raspberries
10 ml/2 tsp lemon or lime juice
30 ml/2 tbsp icing (confectioners') sugar

1 Put the rice in the crock pot and sprinkle the caster sugar over. Split the vanilla pod and scrape the seeds into the crock pot. Add the pod as well.

2 Pour the evaporated milk into a saucepan. Fill the empty can with water and tip into the pan as well. Bring to the boil, then pour over the rice. Stir well, cover and cook on High for 3 hours or Low for 6 hours until thick, creamy and the rice is tender.

3 Meanwhile, to make the coulis, put all the ingredients in a blender or food processor. Run the machine until the mixture is smooth. Tip into a small saucepan and heat through, stirring.

4 Discard the vanilla pod from the crock pot. Spoon the rice into four thick glasses and spoon the raspberry sauce over. Serve hot.

I have used apricots in this dessert, but peaches, nectarines, greengages or plums would all taste fabulous given the same treatment. Somehow the amaretto liqueur, which is based on almonds, brings out the flavour of each of these fruits in a slightly different way. I like to serve them warm, but you could equally well chill them, if you prefer.

poached apricots
in amaretto

SERVES 4

100 g/4 oz/½ cup unrefined caster
  (superfine) sugar
300 ml/½ pt/1¼ cups water
450 g/1 lb fresh apricots, halved and
  stoned (pitted)

60 ml/4 tbsp amaretto

TO SERVE:
Pouring cream

1 Put the sugar and water in a pan and heat gently, stirring, until the sugar dissolves. Bring to the boil.

2 Put the fruit in the crock pot. Pour the boiling sugar syrup over, cover and cook on Low for 2 hours.

3 Add the amaretto, allow to cool slightly, then turn into a glass dish and leave to cool a little more. Serve warm with pouring cream.

SEPTEMBER

This is the time of year when hedgerows and woods are abundant with free food. You'll find plump, juicy, purple elderberries; fragrant ruby rosehips, packed with vitamin C; wonderful wild mushrooms (but make sure you know what you're picking or buy them from a farmer's market or your local supermarket); nuts, blackberries and lots more.

Vegetables

Aubergines (eggplants)
Beetroot (red beets)
Broccoli (calabrese)
Butternut squash
Cardoons
Carrots
Celery
Chillies
Courgettes (zucchini)
Cucumbers
Curly kale
Florence fennel
Garlic
Globe artichokes
Horseradish
Kohl rabi
Leeks
Lettuces
Mangetout (snow peas)
Marrow
Onions
(Bell) peppers
Potatoes (old, maincrop)
Radishes
Rocket (arugula)
Sweetcorn
Swiss chard
Watercress
Wild mushrooms (blewits, ceps, chanterelles, field, horse, oyster, parasol, puffballs)

Fruit and nuts

Apples (Discovery, Russets, Worcester)
Avocados (Hass)
Blackberries
Chestnuts
Clementines
Cranberries
Damsons
Elderberries
Figs
Grapes
Greengages
Hazelnuts (filberts)
Mangoes
Melons
Nectarines
Papaya (paw paw)
Peaches
Pears (William)
Plums
Rosehips
Tomatoes

Meat, poultry and game

Duck
Goose
Grouse
Guinea fowl
Lamb
Quail
Rabbit

Venison
Wild duck (mallard)
Wood pigeon

Fish and seafood

Bream
Brown shrimp
Clams
Cod
Crabs
Dublin bay prawns (scampi)
Grey mullet
Haddock
Halibut
John Dory
Lemon sole
Lobster
Mackerel
Monkfish
Plaice
River trout (brown, rainbow)
Scallops
Sea bass
Skate
Squid
Turbot

Produce in *italics* is UK seasonal fare at its peak.

This recipe has a wonderful flavour of the Mediterranean and, literally, of the sea! If you buy the upper fillets, they will have grey spotted skin, which will need to be removed before rolling; the white skin from the under fillets need not be discarded. Placing the pepper in a plastic bag while it is still hot allows it to sweat, which makes removing the skin much easier.

plaice stuffed with minced squid and red pepper

SERVES 4

1 red (bell) pepper
225 g/8 oz cleaned squid tubes or rings
2 garlic clove, peeled
Salt and freshly ground black pepper
4 plaice fillets, skinned, if necessary, and halved
60 ml/4 tbsp olive oil

50 g/2 oz/¼ cup unsalted (sweet) butter
15 ml/1 tbsp lemon juice
30 ml/2 tbsp chopped fresh parsley

TO SERVE:
Crusty bread and a green salad

1   Toast the pepper all over either under the grill (broiler) or speared on a fork over a gas flame. When blackened and blistering in places, place the pepper in a plastic bag and leave it to cool, then peel off the skin. Halve the pepper and discard the stalk and seeds.

2   Mince (grind) or finely chop in a food processor with the squid and one of the garlic cloves and season well.

3   Spread the stuffing over the skin sides of the fillets and roll up. Place, flap-sides down, in the crock pot.

4   Heat the oil and butter with the lemon juice in a small saucepan or in the microwave until the butter melts. Pour over the fillets and add the other garlic clove, cut in half. Cover and cook on Low for 1 hour.

5   Transfer the plaice rolls to warm shallow dishes and spoon the cooking juices over, discarding the garlic halves. Sprinkle with the parsley and serve with crusty bread and a green salad.

The lovely mix of vegetables in this casserole goes so well with the venison. The dish takes on a Mediterranean feel with the addition of tomatoes, wine and peppers, and though you may think it is odd to have anchovies in it they melt as they cook to impart an amazing richness and depth of flavour to the sauce. Use beef instead of venison, if you prefer.

braised venison with butternut squash and peppers

SERVES 4

25 g/1 oz/¼ cup plain (all-purpose) flour
Salt and freshly ground black pepper
700 g/1½ lb venison, cut into large cubes
30 ml/2 tbsp olive oil
1 onion, chopped
50 g/2 oz smoked lardons (diced bacon)
1 red (bell) pepper, diced
1 green pepper, diced
1 small butternut squash, diced
1 celery stick, diced
1 carrot, diced
1 garlic clove, crushed
400 g/14 oz/1 large can of chopped tomatoes

300 ml/½ pt/1¼ cups beef stock
150 ml/¼ pt/⅔ cup red wine
15 ml/1 tbsp tomato purée (paste)
4 canned anchovy fillets, drained and chopped, or 10 ml/2 tsp anchovy essence (extract)
1 bouquet garni sachet
A good pinch of unrefined caster (superfine) sugar
15 ml/1 tbsp chopped fresh parsley to garnish

TO SERVE:
Creamed potatoes

1   Mix the flour with a little salt and pepper and use to coat the venison.

2   Heat half the oil in a large frying pan. Add the onion and fry quickly for 2 minutes until lightly golden. Transfer to the crock pot with a draining spoon.

3   Heat the remaining oil, add the venison and lardons and fry quickly on all sides to brown. Transfer to the crock pot with a draining spoon, sprinkling over any remaining flour. Add all the prepared vegetables and stir well.

4 Pour the can of tomatoes, the stock and wine into the frying pan and stir in the tomato purée and anchovies. Add the bouquet garni. Bring to the boil, stirring, and season with the sugar and a little salt and pepper. Pour over the venison mixture, stir, cover and cook on High for 4–5 hours or Low for 8–10 hours until the meat and vegetables are tender.

5 Discard the bouquet garni, taste and re-season, if necessary. Sprinkle with the parsley and serve with creamed potatoes.

You can use other oily fish for this recipe when is season but mackerel, being cheap and so delicious, is the perfect one to choose. Look out for the gnarled chunks of fresh horseradish, but if you can't find any, you can buy jars of ready-grated that will do instead. Most of the cooking liquid should have been absorbed at the end of step 1, but it should not be completely dry.

mackerel with spicy horseradish rub and chick peas

SERVES 4

225 g/8 oz/1⅓ cups chick peas
   (garbanzos), soaked in cold water
   for several hours or overnight
900 ml/1½ pts/3¾ cups boiling water
10 ml/2 tsp grated fresh horseradish
10 ml/2 tsp ground cumin
5 ml/1 tsp paprika
2.5 ml/½ tsp salt
4 small mackerel, cleaned
15 g/½ oz/1 tbsp butter

1 onion, finely chopped
2 carrots, finely chopped
1 green (bell) pepper, finely chopped
120 ml/4 fl oz/½ cup chicken or
   vegetable stock
60 ml/4 tbsp chopped fresh parsley
1 garlic clove, crushed

TO SERVE:
Crusty bread and a green salad

1 Drain the chick peas and place in a pan with the boiling water. Bring to the boil and boil rapidly for 10 minutes. Tip into the crock pot, cover and cook on High for 3–4 hours or Low for 6–8 hours until tender.

2 Meanwhile, mix the horseradish with the cumin, paprika and salt. Rinse the fish thoroughly and pat dry on kitchen paper (paper towels). Make several slashes on both sides of the fish and rub the horseradish mixture all over them, inside and out, rubbing well into the slits.

3 Melt the butter in a pan, add the onion, carrots and chopped pepper and fry, stirring, for 2–3 minutes until the vegetables are soft but not brown.

4 Add the stock, bring to the boil and boil for 2 minutes. Stir into the chick peas with half the parsley and the garlic. Lay the fish on top, cover and cook on Low for 2 hours until the fish is tender.

5 Transfer the fish and chick pea mixture to warm plates. Serve hot, sprinkled with the remaining parsley, with crusty bread and a green salad.

This is a lovely change from the more traditional duck with orange, and it's such a good thing to use the plums that will be so abundant and so delicious right now. The sage gives added fragrance and, when served with plain new potatoes and a green vegetable such as mangetout, this becomes a delicious easy-to-make meal for any special occasion.

duck in red wine
and plum sauce

SERVES 4

4 duck portions
10 ml/2 tsp chopped fresh sage
5 firm but ripe plums
200 ml/7 fl oz/scant 1 cup chicken
   stock
200 ml/7 fl oz/scant 1 cup red wine
15 ml/1 tbsp soy sauce

30 ml/2 tbsp plum jam (conserve)
60 ml/4 tbsp cornflour (cornstarch)
60 ml/4 tbsp water
Salt and freshly ground black pepper
4 small sprigs of fresh sage to
   garnish

1   Heat a large heavy-based frying pan. Turn down the heat to moderate, add the duck, skin-sides down, and fry gently until the fat runs, then turn up the heat and brown the duck all over. Transfer the duck to the crock pot and add the sage.

2   Quarter and stone (pit) four of the plums and add to the crock pot.

3   Pour off the excess fat from the frying pan. Add the stock, wine, soy sauce and jam and bring to the boil, stirring, until the jam melts. Blend the cornflour with the water and stir in. Season to taste, then pour over the duck. Cover and cook on High for 2–3 hours or Low for 4–6 hours until tender.

4   Spoon off any fat from the cooking juices in the crock pot. Taste and re-season.

5   Cut the remaining plum into 8 slices, discarding the stone. Transfer the duck to warm plates and spoon the sauce around. Garnish each piece of duck with a small sprig of sage and two slices of plum and serve hot.

This is a traditionally British way of serving marrow. It's so easy but also very satisfying and tasty. You could experiment with adding extra flavours such as tomato purée and a little hot chilli powder – even some red kidney beans – to make the filling more like a chilli con carne but, in my opinion, the excellence of the dish lies in its simplicity.

stuffed marrow
with beef and carrots

SERVES 4

1 onion, chopped
350 g/12 oz minced (ground) beef
2 carrots, grated
300 ml/½ pt/1¼ cups beef stock
1 bay leaf
Salt and freshly ground black pepper
1 egg, beaten
A little butter for greasing
60 ml/4 tbsp plain (all-purpose) flour

1 small marrow, peeled, sliced into 6
  rings and seeded
90 ml/6 tbsp water
15 ml/1 tbsp chopped fresh parsley
  to garnish

TO SERVE:
Plain boiled potatoes

1 Put the onion, beef and carrots in a frying pan. Fry, stirring, until the grains of meat are separate and browned. Add the stock, bay leaf and a little salt and pepper. Bring to the boil, reduce the heat and simmer for 5 minutes. Discard the bay leaf, taste and re-season, if necessary. Drain off the stock and reserve. Beat in the egg.

2 Grease a large crock pot and place the marrow rings in it. Spoon the beef mixture into the cavities in the marrow and press down well. (If necessary, put as many rings in the crock pot as will fit and fill them, then grease a piece of foil on both sides and lay on top, with the edges folded up to form a tray, and add the remaining marrow rings and fill with the remaining stuffing.)

3 Pour the reserved stock around the marrow (with some on the top layer, if necessary). Cover and cook on High for 2 hours or Low for 4 hours until tender.

4 Whisk the flour and water in a small saucepan. Transfer the marrow to warm serving plates and keep warm. Whisk the cooking stock into the flour mixture, bring to the boil and cook, stirring, for 2 minutes until thickened. Season to taste. Spoon the gravy over the marrow, garnish with the parsley and serve with potatoes.

Elderberries are popular for making home-made wine, but you may not know that they are also wonderful for flavouring apples. The easiest way to strip the berries from their stalks is between the prongs of a fork (this works for currants too). You can use a strip of lemon zest instead of a cinnamon stick. Try using blackberries instead but omit the lemon altogether.

elderberry and apple compôte

SERVES 4

100 g/4 oz elderberries, removed from their stalks
2 large Bramley cooking (tart) apples, peeled, quartered and cored
75 g/3 oz/⅓ cup unrefined caster (superfine) sugar

1 piece of cinnamon stick
2.5 ml/½ tsp minced lemon grass (from a jar)
150 ml/¼ pt/⅔ cup boiling water

TO SERVE:
Vanilla ice-cream

1 Pick over the elderberries to remove any last bits of stalk. Place the apples in the crock pot, cored-sides down.

2 Scatter the elderberries over the apples and sprinkle with the sugar. Add the cinnamon stick and lemon grass.

3 Pour the boiling water over, cover and cook on Low for 2 hours.

4 Discard the cinnamon stick and serve hot or cold with vanilla ice-cream.

OCTOBER

Autumn is upon us — dark evenings, dew on the grass, frost at night. Halloween, pumpkins, wild mushrooms, nut and berries all spring to mind. Yellow quinces, great for cooking with apples and making into jelly, are also ripe. Apart from food for free, there is an abundance of home-grown produce — squashes, brassicas, roots, tubers and plenty of fruit. The game season is also well under way and there's lots of fresh fish to choose from.

Vegetables
Aubergines (eggplants)
Beetroot (red beets)
Broccoli (calabrese)
Butternut squash
Cardoons
Carrots
*Cavolo nero (black
   cabbage)*
Celeriac (celery root)
Celery
Chillies
Curly kale
Florence fennel
Globe artichokes
Horseradish
Kohl rabi
Leeks
Lettuces
Marrow
Onions
(Bell) peppers
Potatoes (old, maincrop)
Pumpkins
Radishes
Rocket (arugula)
Swedes (rutabaga)
Sweet potatoes
Swiss chard
Turnips
Watercress
*Wild mushrooms
   (blewits, ceps,*
*chanterelles, field,
   horse, oyster, parasol,
   puffballs)*
Yams

Fruit and nuts
*Apples (Russets, Cox's,
   Bramleys)*
Avocados (Hass)
Chestnuts
Damsons
Figs
Grapes
Hazelnuts (filberts)
Papaya (paw paw)
*Pears (Comice,
   Conference)*
Quinces
Raspberries (late crop)
Rosehips
Tomatoes
Walnuts

Meat, poultry and game
Duck
Goose
Grouse
Guinea fowl
Hare
Lamb
Partridge
Pheasant
Rabbit
Snipe
Venison
Wild duck (mallard)
Woodcock
Wood pigeon

Fish and seafood
Bream
Brill
Brown shrimp
Clams
Crabs
Dublin bay prawns
   (scampi)
Eels
Grey mullet
Haddock
Hake
Halibut
John Dory
Lemon sole
Lobster
Mackerel
Monkfish
Mussels
Oysters
Plaice
*River trout (brown,
   rainbow)*
Scallops
Sea bass
Squid
Turbot

Produce in *italics* is UK seasonal fare at its peak.

If you can't get enough wild mushrooms, use some cultivated ones as well to make up the weight. The flavour won't be quite as good but it will still be a very special dish indeed. The garlic crostini make a lovely bed for the mushrooms but, for a more informal meal or to save time, you could omit them and just serve the soup in the normal way.

wild mushroom soup on garlic crostini

SERVES 4

25 g/1 oz/2 tbsp butter
1 onion, finely chopped
350 g/12 oz wild mushrooms, trimmed and roughly chopped (not too small)
30 ml/2 tbsp plain (all-purpose) flour
60 ml/4 tbsp cold water
5 ml/1 tsp tomato purée (paste)
600 ml/1 pt/2½ cups chicken or vegetable stock

15 ml/1 tbsp brandy
1 bouquet garni sachet
Salt and freshly ground black pepper

FOR THE GARLIC CROSTINI:
1 garlic clove
4 slices of ciabatta bread
45 ml/3 tbsp olive oil
15 ml/1 tbsp chopped fresh parsley to garnish

1 Melt the butter in a saucepan, add the onion and fry gently for 1 minute, stirring. Stir in the mushrooms, then tip into the crock pot.

2 Blend the flour with the water and tomato purée. Stir into the saucepan and gradually blend in the stock and brandy. Bring to the boil, stirring, and pour into the crock pot. Add the bouquet garni and some salt and pepper. Cover and cook on High for 2 hours or Low for 4 hours until the mushrooms are really tender and the soup is full of flavour and thickened slightly (it will sit happily for at least an hour longer).

3 Meanwhile, to make the crostini, cut the garlic in half and rub all over both sides of the bread. Heat the oil in a frying pan, throw in the garlic clove and fry the bread on both sides until golden. Discard the garlic clove and drain the slices on kitchen paper (paper towels).

4 Discard the bouquet garni from the soup, taste and re-season if necessary. Place the crostini in four warm open soup plates. Spoon the mushrooms on top, using a draining spoon, then pour the soup around. Garnish with the parsley and serve straight away.

This very easy dish is based on the cuisine of Provence in France, where the outstanding flavours come from the tomatoes, olives, capers and herbs of the region. Here thick, meaty monkfish is gently slow cooked in a tomato sauce well spiked with all these ingredients. You can use another, cheaper, meaty white fish, if you prefer.

monkfish with rich tomato and caper sauce

SERVES 4

30 ml/2 tbsp olive oil
1 large onion, finely chopped
2 celery sticks, finely chopped
2 garlic cloves, crushed
4 beefsteak tomatoes, skinned and
  chopped
150 ml/¼ pt/⅔ cup dry white wine
45 ml/3 tbsp tomato purée (paste)
2.5 ml/½ tsp dried herbes de
  Provence
4 small thick pieces of monkfish
  fillet, about 150 g/5 oz each

50 g/2 oz black olives, stoned
  (pitted), if preferred
10 ml/2 tsp pickled capers
Salt and freshly ground black pepper
30 ml/2 tbsp chopped fresh parsley
  to garnish

TO SERVE:
Plain boiled rice and a green salad

1   Heat the oil in a frying pan, add the onion, celery and garlic and fry gently, stirring, for 5 minutes until softened but not browned. Add the tomatoes, wine, tomato purée and herbs and bring to the boil.

2   Put the fish in the crock pot. Add the tomato mixture and scatter the olives and capers over. Season lightly. Cover and cook on Low for 2 hours until everything is tender.

3   Taste and re-season if necessary. Serve spooned over a bed of rice and sprinkled with the parsley with a green salad.

Grouse is a lovely game bird, full of flavour and not too tough! I love it as here, casseroled with some seasonal root vegetables, wine and cream. As a variation, you could make it using cider and two sliced Cox's apples instead of the wine and mushrooms; the result would be reminiscent of a classic Normandy dish usually made with pheasant.

grouse with turnips, mushrooms and white wine

SERVES 4

40 g/1½ oz/3 tbsp butter
2 oven-ready grouse, halved
100 g/4 oz whole baby button
   mushrooms
1 large onion, chopped
4 turnips, diced
25 g/1 oz/¼ cup plain (all-purpose)
   flour
200 ml/7 fl oz/scant 1 cup chicken
   stock
200 ml/7 fl oz/scant 1 cup medium-
   dry white wine

1 bouquet garni sachet
Salt and freshly ground black pepper
60 ml/4 tbsp double (heavy) cream
15 ml/1 tbsp chopped fresh parsley
   to garnish

TO SERVE:
Creamed potatoes and buttered
   cabbage

1   Melt 25 g/1 oz/2 tbsp of the butter in a saucepan, add the grouse and brown on all sides. Transfer to the crock pot with a draining spoon and add the mushrooms.

2   Melt the remaining butter in the pan, add the onion and turnips and fry, stirring, for 2 minutes. Stir in the flour and cook for 1 minute, stirring all the time. Bend in the stock and wine and bring to the boil, stirring, until thickened. Pour over the grouse.

3   Add the bouquet garni and a little salt and pepper. Cover and cook on High for 3 hours or Low for 6 hours until really tender.

4   Carefully lift the grouse out of the slow cooker and transfer to warm serving plates. Discard the bouquet garni and stir the cream into the sauce. Taste and re-season if necessary. Spoon the sauce over the birds and garnish with the parsley, then serve with creamed potatoes and buttered cabbage.

This is a lovely accompaniment to grilled meat, chicken or sausages or try it with some poached eggs and, perhaps, some wilted spinach. For a complete vegetarian meal, stir in two drained cans of chick peas before you start cooking (or cook some dried ones in the slow cooker first, as on page 92). Try it with other squashes such as pumpkin or marrow too.

seeded spiced butternut squash

SERVES 4–6

2 butternut squashes, about 700 g/ 1½ lb in total
30 ml/2 tbsp sunflower oil
1 large onion, halved and thinly sliced
15 ml/1 tbsp caraway seeds
15 ml/1 tbsp cumin seeds
15 ml/1 tbsp black mustard seeds

2.5 ml/½ tsp ground turmeric
2.5 ml/½ tsp hot chilli powder
2.5 ml/½ tsp salt
5 ml/1 tsp unrefined light brown sugar
150 ml/¼ pt/⅔ cup water
2 small bay leaves
30 ml/2 tbsp pumpkin seeds

1 Peel and seed the squashes and cut the flesh into bite-sized chunks.

2 Heat the oil in a frying pan, add the onion and fry, stirring, for 4 minutes until lightly golden. Stir in the caraway, cumin and mustard seeds and cook until they start to 'pop'.

3 Add the turmeric and chilli powder and stir for 30 seconds. Add the salt, sugar and water and bring to the boil.

4 Put the squash in the crock pot with the bay leaves and pour the spicy sauce over. Cover and cook on High for 2 hours or Low for 4 hours until tender.

5 Discard the bay leaves, stir gently and serve sprinkled with the pumpkin seeds.

If you have a fig tree there will be loads of figs that plump up a bit but don't quite ripen into sweet, fat purple baubles. Slow cooked in a syrup flavoured with lime zest, they make a delicious dessert to serve either hot or cold. It doesn't work with the little green bullets though! If you have a glut, cook them all and freeze them for future use.

zested green figs
with greek yoghurt

SERVES 4

16 fairly plump green figs
175 g/6 oz/¾ cup unrefined caster
  (superfine) sugar
Thinly pared zest of half a lime

300 ml/½ pt/1¼ cups boiling water

TO SERVE:
Greek-style plain yoghurt

1 Put the figs in the crock pot with the sugar, lime zest and boiling water.

2 Cover and cook on Low for 3–4 hours until tender (the time will depend on how ripe the figs were). Leave to cool in the syrup, then chill.

3 Serve with Greek-style plain yoghurt.

This lovely dish has a wonderful flavour and a hint of spice. You don't have to stick with just 6 pears – you could cook as many as you can fit into the dish with the same amount of syrup. Serve them hot or cold with a dollop of fluffy whipped cream. I like to accompany them with some thin crisp biscuits, such as almond thins or, for added luxury, some Florentines.

spiced pears
in red wine

SERVES 6

6 fairly ripe pears, peeled but left
   whole
2 cloves
1 piece of cinnamon stick

1 star anise
600 ml/1 pt/2½ cups red wine
175 g/6 oz/¾ cup unrefined caster
   (superfine) sugar

1 Stand the pears in a dish that will hold the pears snugly and fit in a large crock pot. Tuck the spices around.

2 Bring the wine to the boil in a saucepan with the sugar, stirring until dissolved. Pour over the pears. Cover and cook on Low for 2–3 hours until tender, basting once during cooking to coat evenly in the wine syrup.

3 Leave to cool, then chill. Discard the spices before serving.

This liqueur has a lovely autumnal orangey-red colour when clear. It is absolutely delicious poured over lots of ice, or try a measure mixed with orange or apple juice. Alternatively, for a cocktail I've named Vinca Rose, *add a good dash to some chilled sparkling white wine; because rosehips are packed with Vitamin C, I like to kid myself I've created a healthy tonic!*

rosehip
liqueur

MAKES ABOUT 600 ML/1 PT/2½ CUPS

100 g/4 oz bright red rosehips
100 g/4 oz/½ cup unrefined caster (superfine) sugar

150 ml/¼ pt/⅔ cup boiling water
450 ml/¾ pt/2 cups vodka
1.5 ml/¼ tsp citric acid

1 Roughly crush the rosehips briefly in a food processor or pound in a bowl with the end of a rolling pin. Tip into the crock pot and add the sugar and water. Cover and cook on Low for 4 hours.

2 Remove the crock pot from the base and stir in the vodka. Leave to cool, then stir in the citric acid. Strain through a jelly bag or a sieve (strainer) lined with a new disposable kitchen cloth, then filter the liquid through a double thickness of kitchen paper (paper towel) or a coffee filter paper to remove the fine fibres in the rosehips.

3 Pour into a clean screw-topped bottle, then store in a cool, dark place until completely clear (this may take several weeks). Ideally, leave it for several months to mature.

NOVEMBER

Bonfire night, roasted chestnuts, baked potatoes and warm comforting food like stews and casseroles epitomise the month. Winter is upon us and there are plenty of home-grown fruits and vegetables around to cheer us, from apples and pears galore to lovely dark green kale, cavolo nero, celeriac and all the lovely squashes from pumpkins to marrows. Seafood abounds and there should be plenty of game, if you like it.

Vegetables	Fruit and nuts	Fish and seafood
Beetroot (red beets)	*Apples (Russets, Cox's,*	Bream
Butternut squash	*Bramleys)*	Brill
Cabbages (green, red,	Avocados (Fuerte, Hass)	Clams
white)	*Chestnuts*	*Cod*
Cardoons	Cranberries	*Crabs*
Cavolo nero (black	Dates	Dublin bay prawns
cabbage)	*Medlars*	(scampi)
Celeriac (celery root)	Pears (Comice,	*Haddock*
Celery	Conference)	Hake
Chicory (Belgian endive)	Persimmons	John Dory
Curly kale	*Quinces*	Lemon sole
Jerusalem artichokes	*Raspberries (late crop)*	*Lobster*
Kohl rabi	*Sloes*	Monkfish
Leeks	*Walnuts*	*Mussels*
Lettuces		Oysters
Parsnips	**Meat, poultry and game**	Plaice
Potatoes (old, maincrop)	Duck	*Scallops*
Pumpkin	*Goose*	*Sea bass*
Salsify and scorzonera	*Grouse*	*Squid*
Shallots	*Guinea fowl*	Turbot
Swedes (rutabaga)	*Hare*	
Sweet potatoes	*Partridge*	
Swiss chard	*Pheasant*	
Turnips	*Rabbit*	
Watercress	*Snipe*	
White truffles	*Venison*	
Wild mushrooms	Woodcock	
(blewits, horse,	*Wood pigeon*	
oyster)		

Produce in *italics* is UK seasonal fare at its peak.

Based on the French classic vichysoisse, *this soup is a must in the slow cooker. Always make sure you wash leeks well as the green parts are often gritty. If time allows, a good method is to slit the leeks down their length, leaving them joined at the root end, and standing them upside-down in a jug of water for about half an hour so all the grit falls to the bottom.*

velvet leek and potato soup with crème fraîche

SERVES 4

15 g/½ oz/1 tbsp butter
1 onion, chopped
45 ml/3 tbsp plain (all-purpose) flour
750 ml/1¼ pt/3 cups chicken or
   vegetable stock
2 leeks, trimmed and chopped

2 potatoes, peeled and diced
1 bouquet garni sachet
Salt and freshly ground black pepper
150 ml/¼ pt/⅔ cup crème fraîche,
   plus extra to garnish
15 ml/1 tbsp chopped fresh parsley

1 Melt the butter in a saucepan, add the onion and fry gently, stirring, for 2 minutes until softened but not browned.

2 Stir in the flour, then gradually blend in the stock and bring to the boil, stirring all the time.

3 Put the leeks and potatoes in the crock pot. Pour on the thickened liquid, add the bouquet garni and a little salt and pepper. Cover and cook on High for 2–3 hours or Low for 4–6 hours until everything is tender.

4 Discard the bouquet garni and transfer the soup to a blender or food processor. Add the crème fraîche, then purée until smooth. Taste and re-season, if necessary.

5 Pour back in the crock pot and reheat for 5–10 minutes. Ladle into warm bowls and serve with a swirl of crème fraîche and a sprinkling of chopped parsley.

Terrines cook beautifully in the slow cooker and use far less fuel than when they are cooked conventionally in the oven. I have used blanched cabbage leaves to line the dish, but if you prefer you could use rashers of rinded streaky bacon instead. You could also substitute chicken thigh meat and chicken livers for the pork mixture for a change.

coarse pork terrine
with sage and apple

SERVES 6–12

4–6 large outer green cabbage
  leaves
1 onion, quartered
2 garlic cloves
A small handful of fresh parsley
15 ml/1 tbsp chopped fresh sage, or
  5 ml/1 tsp dried
450 g/1 lb belly pork slices, rinded
  and any bones removed
100 g/4 oz unsmoked bacon pieces,
  trimmed of any rind or gristle

350 g/12 oz pigs' liver, trimmed
2 Cox's apples, peeled and cored
1.5 ml/¼ tsp ground mace
60 ml/4 tbsp dry cider
7.5 ml/1½ tsp salt
Freshly ground black pepper

TO SERVE:
Crusty bread, mustard and a side
salad

1   Trim the thick stalks from the cabbage. Blanch the leaves in boiling water for 2 minutes, then drain, rinse with cold water and drain again. Pat them dry on kitchen paper (paper towels). Line a 1.5 litre/2½ pt/6 cup terrine or large loaf tin with some of the leaves, letting the edges flop over the sides of the container.

2   Using a food processor or coarse mincer (grinder), process the onion, garlic, herbs, pork, bacon, liver and apples fairly coarsely.

3   Mix in the mace, cider, salt and a good grinding of pepper. Turn into the prepared dish and level the surface.

4   Fold the leaves over and top with the remaining leaves to cover the meat mixture completely. Cover with greaseproof (waxed) paper, then a lid or foil and stand the terrine in the crock pot. Pour 2.5 cm/1 in of boiling water around.

5   Cover and cook on High for 3 hours or Low for 6 hours until cooked through, any juices are clear and the terrine is firm to the touch.

6   Remove from the crock pot and uncover. Top with some clean greaseproof paper and weight down with heavy weights or cans of food. Leave until cold, then chill.

7   Loosen the edges and turn out on to a serving plate or board. Serve sliced with crusty bread, mustard and a side salad.

This is one of my favourite ways of serving big open field mushrooms – their flavour is just out of this world. If you aren't lucky enough to find field mushrooms, you can use large home-grown organic open cultivated ones. The flavour won't be quite as good but still well worth trying. I recommend lots of fresh crusty bread to mop up the juices.

wild mushrooms
with garlic and cider

SERVES 4

25 g/1 oz/2 tbsp butter
4 very large or 8 large flat field
    mushrooms, peeled and stalks
    removed and reserved
2 large garlic cloves, finely chopped
150 ml/¼ pt/⅔ cup dry cider
150 ml/¼ pt/⅔ cup double (heavy)
    cream

Salt and freshly ground black pepper
30 ml/2 tbsp chopped fresh parsley
    to garnish

TO SERVE:
Crusty bread

1   Smear the butter over the base of a large crock pot. Lay the mushrooms caps in the pot.

2   Chop the stalks and scatter over the caps with the garlic.

3   Place the cider and cream in a small saucepan and bring just to the boil. Pour over the mushrooms and season well. Cover and cook on Low for 3–4 hours, or even longer for a more intense flavour.

4   Carefully lift out the mushrooms with a fish slice and transfer to warm, shallow dishes. Taste and re-season the juices, if necessary. Spoon over the mushrooms and sprinkle with the parsley. Serve hot with crusty bread.

Chicory is delicious braised. Here I've wrapped it in ham (reminiscent of a Belgian speciality where it's coated in a cheese sauce) but I've gently cooked them in a tomato sauce, then added a crunchy cheese topping that's placed briefly under the grill to melt it. This makes a delicious starter, or a satisfying light lunch with the addition of some crusty bread.

cheese and tomato topped chicory ham wraps

SERVES 4

4 heads of chicory (Belgian endive)
8 slices of sweet-cured ham
15 ml/1 tbsp pickled capers, chopped
15 ml/1 tbsp snipped fresh chives
400 g/14 oz/1 large can of chopped tomatoes

15 ml/1 tbsp tomato purée (paste)
A good pinch of unrefined caster (superfine) sugar
Salt and freshly ground black pepper
75 g/3 oz/¾ cup grated Gruyère (Swiss) cheese
25 g/1 oz/½ cup cornflakes, crushed

1 Cut a cone shape out of the base of each head of chicory. Cut into halves. Blanch in boiling water for 2 minutes, drain well, then wrap each in a slice of ham and lay them in a shallow flameproof dish that will fit in the slow cooker. Add about 5 mm/¼ in of boiling water to the crock pot.

2 Mix the capers with the chives, tomatoes and tomato purée in a saucepan and bring to the boil. Season to taste with the sugar, salt and pepper.

3 Pour over the chicory, cover and cook on High for 1 hour or Low for 2 hours until the chicory is tender.

4 Remove the dish from the crock pot. Mix the cheese with the cornflakes and sprinkle all over the surface. Place under a preheated grill (broiler) for 3–4 minutes until the cheese melts and bubbles and is beginning to turn lightly golden. Serve hot.

Sun-blush tomatoes are semi-dried and have an intense flavour. They make a great antipasti when served with some sliced salami and cubes of real buffalo Mozzarella cheese. If you can only find baby squid, use 8–12 instead of the 4 larger ones. I love the flavour combination of squid with chillies, but you can omit the chillies if you like a more delicate flavour.

whole squid with chillies and sun-blush tomatoes

SERVES 4

120 ml/4 fl oz/½ cup olive oil
1 onion, very finely chopped
2 garlic cloves, crushed
4 largish squid, cleaned
30 ml/2 tbsp chopped fresh parsley, plus a little extra to garnish
2.5 ml/½ tsp dried oregano
Salt and freshly ground black pepper
15 ml/1 tbsp lemon juice

1 fat red chilli, seeded and thinly sliced
1 fat green chilli, seeded and thinly sliced
25 g/1 oz sun-blush tomatoes, roughly chopped

TO SERVE:
Crusty bread and a green salad

1   Pour the oil into the crock pot, add the onion and garlic, cover and cook on High for 1 hour.

2   Meanwhile, rinse the squid and pat dry on kitchen paper (paper towels). Chop the tentacles, discarding the hard core in the centre.

3   When the onion and garlic have finished cooking, add the squid and all the remaining ingredients to the crock pot. Cover and cook on Low for 2 hours until the squid is tender and succulent.

4   Taste and re-season if necessary. Transfer the squid and juices to warm shallow dishes, sprinkle with a little extra chopped parsley and serve hot with lots of crusty bread and a green salad.

This is one of my favourite dishes and one I return to time and time again. The potatoes are creamy and soft and the fish firm and meaty. You can, of course, use other fish than haddock if you like. The addition of truffle oil adds flavour to the mushrooms and a touch of luxury. Instead of creamy milk, you could use half milk and half single cream.

haddock with oyster mushrooms, potatoes and truffle oil

SERVES 4

450 g/1 lb potatoes, peeled
15 g/½ oz/1 tbsp unsalted (sweet) butter
1 onion, finely chopped
2 rashers (slices) of unsmoked streaky bacon, snipped into very small pieces
30 ml/2 tbsp dry vermouth
200 ml/7 fl oz/scant 1 cup creamy milk
Salt and freshly ground black pepper

100 g/4 oz oyster mushrooms, roughly cut up
15 ml/1 tbsp truffle oil
5 ml/1 tsp lemon juice
4 pieces of haddock loin, about 150 g/5 oz each
30 ml/2 tbsp chopped fresh parsley to garnish

TO SERVE:
A green salad

1 Slice the potatoes as thinly as possible, preferably with a mandolin or in a food processor.

2 Melt the butter in a saucepan, add the onion and bacon and fry gently, stirring, for 2 minutes until the onion is soft but only just turning lightly golden.

3 Add the vermouth and boil rapidly until almost evaporated. Add the milk and bring to the boil.

4 Put the potatoes in the crock pot. Pour the contents of the saucepan over and stir gently. Season well. Cover and cook on Low for 3–4 hours until tender.

5 Mix the mushrooms with the truffle oil, lemon juice and a little salt and pepper. Lay the fish on top of the potatoes and pile the mushroom mixture on top of each piece. Cover and cook on Low for a further 1 hour until tender.

6 Carefully transfer the potatoes with the fish to warm plates, sprinkle with the parsley and serve with a green salad.

Hare has quite a strong, gamey flavour. It can be quite hard to find even at this time of year, but you could use pheasant, rabbit, venison or beef instead for an equally rich, sumptuous and satisfying casserole. However, rabbit will take only 2–3 hours on High or 4–6 hours on Low. If using pieces of beef or venison, allow 175 g/6 oz per person.

hare with brown ale, prunes and mustard

SERVES 4–6

60 ml/4 tbsp plain (all-purpose) flour
Salt and freshly ground black pepper
1 oven-ready hare, cut into 6 joints
45 ml/3 tbsp sunflower oil
100 g/4 oz button mushrooms, sliced
100 g/4 oz ready-to-eat prunes, halved and stoned (pitted)
1 bay leaf
15 g/½ oz/1 tbsp butter
1 onion, chopped
1 celery stick, chopped

10 ml/2 tsp Dijon mustard
250 ml/8 fl oz/1 cup brown ale or stout
150 ml/¼ pt/⅔ cup strong beef stock
5 ml/1 tsp unrefined light brown sugar
5 ml/1 tsp coarse sea salt

TO SERVE:
Fluffy mashed potatoes and curly kale

1 Mix the flour with a little salt and pepper and use to coat the hare joints.

2 Heat half the oil in a frying pan, add the hare joints and brown on all sides. Transfer to the crock pot with a draining spoon and add the mushrooms and prunes. Tuck in the bay leaf.

3 Add the remaining oil and the butter to the frying pan, add the onion and celery and fry, stirring, for 3 minutes until lightly golden.

4 Stir in any remaining flour, the mustard, brown ale or stout, stock, sugar and salt and bring to the boil, stirring all the time. Pour over the hare. Cover and cook on High for 4–5 hours or Low for 8–10 hours until meltingly tender.

5 Discard the bay leaf, taste and re-season, if necessary. Serve with fluffy mashed potatoes and curly kale.

Fresh chestnuts are fiddly to prepare but it's worth setting aside the time to do double the quantity, then freezing half for another time. Cooking them in the slow cooker ensures they don't boil dry (something that I'm prone to do). You can cheat and use a large can of unsweetened chestnut purée but that would rather defeat the point of using seasonal produce!

chestnut torte
with shiny chocolate ganache

SERVES 8–10

FOR THE TORTE:
450 g/1 lb chestnuts
200 ml/7 fl oz/scant 1 cup milk
100 g /4 oz/½ cup unsalted (sweet) butter, plus a little extra for greasing
175 g/6 oz plain (semi-sweet) chocolate with 70 per cent cocoa solids
225 g/8 oz/1⅓ cups icing (confectioners') sugar, sifted

4 eggs, separated
5 ml/1 tsp vanilla essence (extract)

FOR THE GANACHE:
100 g/4 oz plain chocolate with 70 per cent cocoa solids
120 ml/4 fl oz/½ cup double (heavy) cream

1 To make the torte, cut a slit in the skin of each chestnut. Place in the crock pot and just cover with boiling water. Cover and cook on High for 1 hour.

2 Lift the chestnuts out of the slow cooker with a draining spoon and plunge into cold water. When completely cold, peel off the hard shell and scrape off the soft brown inner skin. Drop the chestnuts into a blender or food processor, add the milk and purée until smooth.

3 Grease a 20 cm/8 in springform cake tin and line the base with baking parchment. Place the tin in a sheet of foil and press it up the side of the tin (to prevent water seeping in).

4 Break up the chocolate and place it in a bowl. Stand the bowl in a saucepan of simmering water and stir until melted. Alternatively, melt briefly in the microwave.

5   Beat the butter and icing sugar until light and fluffy, then beat in the chestnut purée, the egg yolks, vanilla essence and melted chocolate. Whisk the egg whites until stiff and fold into the chestnut mixture with a metal spoon. Spoon the mixture into the prepared tin and level the surface. Cover the tin with foil, twisting and folding under the rim to secure.

6   Pour about 5 mm/¼ in of boiling water into the crock pot to cover the base. Stand the torte in the pot, cover and cook on Low for 4–5 hours until fairly firm.

7   Remove from the crock pot and leave to cool in the tin.

8   Meanwhile, to make the ganache, break up the chocolate and place it in a clean saucepan with the cream. Heat gently, stirring all the time with a wooden spoon, until thick. Leave to cool slightly until it has a thick, coating consistency.

9   Transfer the cooled torte to a serving plate. Spoon the ganache over, spreading it out with a palette knife so it coats the top and sides of the torte completely. Wipe the edge of the plate to clean up any excess chocolate. Leave to set but do not chill.

Traditional pumpkin pies are pastry-based affairs, baked in the oven. Here I use a biscuit crust and fill it with a lovely sweet spiced pumpkin custard, which is slow cooked until moist and set. When cold, it is smothered in whipped cream and decorated with flakes of bitter chocolate. Instead of rich tea biscuits, you can use any other crisp plain biscuits.

pumpkin pie in a pot

SERVES 8

A little oil for greasing
200 g/7 oz/1 small packet of rich tea biscuits (cookies), crushed
100 g/4 oz/½ cup butter, melted
700 g/1½ lb pumpkin, peeled and diced
175 g/6 oz/⅔ cup unrefined light brown sugar

1.5 ml/¼ tsp ground ginger
1.5 ml/¼ tsp grated nutmeg
A good pinch of ground cloves
3 eggs, beaten
300 ml/½ pt/1¼ cups double (heavy) cream, whipped
A little grated bitter chocolate to decorate

1 Lightly grease a 20 cm/8 in springform cake tin. Place the tin in a sheet of foil and press it up the side of the tin (to prevent water seeping in). Mix the crushed biscuits with the melted butter and press into the base and a little way up the side of the prepared tin.

2 Boil the pumpkin for about 5 minutes in a little water or steam for 10 minutes until very soft. Drain thoroughly, if necessary, then purée in a blender or food processor with the sugar, spices and eggs.

3 Pour the mixture into the prepared tin (it will be very runny). Place in the crock pot and pour round about 5 mm/¼ in of boiling water – enough to cover the base of the pot. Cover and cook on Low for 2 hours until set.

4 Remove from the crock pot and leave to cool, then chill.

5 When ready to serve, carefully remove the pie from the tin and transfer it to a serving plate. Cover the top with the whipped cream and sprinkle with a little grated bitter chocolate.

DECEMBER

Christmas is coming and all those lovely traditional Christmassy foods come into play. Brussels sprouts (not the greatest choice for slow cooking except in my heart-warming soup), sweet-scented citrus (not from the UK but absolutely at their best from hotter climes), nuts, game and, of course, Christmas pudding. You can make a magnificent one in your slow cooker — and no steamy kitchen to endure (nor is it likely to boil dry!). Cranberry sauce for your Christmas turkey is a must in the crock pot and, to round it all off, you can even cook a festive bird in it!

Vegetables
Beetroot
Brussels sprouts
Cabbages (green, red, white)
Cardoons
Carrots
Cauliflowers
Celeriac (celery root)
Celery
Chicory (Belgian endive)
Curly kale
Jerusalem artichokes
Lettuces
Parsnips
Potatoes (old, maincrop)
Pumpkins
Radicchio
Shallots
Swedes (rutabaga)
Sweet potatoes
Swiss chard
Turnips
Watercress

Fruit and nuts
Almonds
Apples (Russets, Cox's, Bramleys)
Avocados (Fuerte)
Chestnuts
Clementines
Cranberries
Dates
Medlars
Passion fruit
Pears (Comice, Conference)
Physalis
Pineapples
Pomegranates
Satsumas
Tangerines
Walnuts

Meat, poultry and game
Duck
Goose
Grouse
Guinea fowl
Hare
Partridge
Pheasant
Rabbit
Snipe
Turkey
Venison
Wild duck (mallard)
Woodcock
Wood pigeon

Fish and seafood
Bream
Brill
Clams
Haddock
Hake
Halibut
John Dory
Lemon sole
Monkfish
Mussels
Oysters
Plaice
Scallops
Sea bass
Turbot

Produce in *italics* is UK seasonal fare at its peak.

The lovely thing about this soup is that you don't have to fiddle around preparing the sprouts in the normal way. Just trim off any brown stumps and that's all – those outer leaves are thrown into the pot with the rest! This is my version of the German speciality called Saxe-Coburg; some say it was created for Queen Victoria's consort, Prince Albert.

creamy brussels sprout soup with ham

SERVES 4–6

2 slices of sweet-cured ham
15 g/½ oz/1 tbsp butter
1 onion, chopped
30 ml/2 tbsp plain (all–purpose) flour
750 ml/1¼ pts/3 cups chicken or vegetable stock
450 g/1 lb Brussels sprouts, trimmed

1 potato, diced
Salt and freshly ground black pepper
A good grating of fresh nutmeg
60 ml/4 tbsp milk
90 ml/6 tbsp double (heavy) cream, plus extra to garnish

1 Tear up one slice of ham and place it in the crock pot. Finely shred the other slice, wrap it in foil and reserve for garnish.

2 Melt the butter in a saucepan, add the onion and fry gently, stirring, for 2 minutes until softened but not browned. Stir in the flour and stock and bring to the boil.

3 Put the sprouts in the crock pot with the potato and pour on the boiling thickened stock mixture. Season with salt, pepper and nutmeg.

4 Cover and cook on High for 2–3 hours or Low for 4–6 hours until really tender.

5 Purée the mixture in a blender or food processor with the milk and the cream, then return to the crock pot on Low until ready to serve.

6 Ladle the soup into bowls and garnish with a swirl of cream and the shredded ham.

This is based on a mouth-watering Spanish speciality that uses chick peas with black pudding and fruit. I love the creamy texture of pearly white haricot beans, which perfectly complement the earthiness of the black pudding and the sweetness of the pears and raisins. Try it for a starter or as a light lunch with the accompaniment of a crisp green salad.

white beans with black pudding, raisins and pears

SERVES 4–6

100 g/4 oz/⅔ cup dried haricot (navy) beans, soaked in cold water for several hours or overnight
450 ml/¾ pt/2 cups boiling water
25 g/1 oz/3 tbsp raisins
2 firm Conference pears, peeled, cored and diced
30 ml/2 tbsp dry white wine
30 ml/2 tbsp olive oil, plus extra for drizzling
1 onion, halved and thinly sliced

45 ml/3 tbsp pine nuts
1 garlic clove, finely chopped
100 g/4 oz black pudding, skinned and diced
1 large sprig of fresh rosemary, finely chopped
45 ml/3 tbsp chopped fresh parsley
Salt and freshly ground black pepper

TO SERVE:
Crusty bread

1 Drain the beans and place in a saucepan with the boiling water. Bring to the boil and boil rapidly for 10 minutes. Tip into the crock pot, cover and cook on High for 2–3 hours or Low for 4–6 hours until tender and most of the liquid has been absorbed.

2 Meanwhile, soak the raisins and pears in the wine for at least 30 minutes until the raisins are plump and most of the wine has been absorbed.

3 Heat the oil in a small saucepan, add the onion and fry gently for 2 minutes to soften. Add the pine nuts and fry, stirring, for 1 minute until lightly golden. Tip the mixture into the cooked beans in the crock pot with the garlic, the soaked raisins and pears, the black pudding, rosemary and half the parsley. Season well. Stir gently, cover and cook on High for 1 hour or Low for 2 hours.

4 Taste the mixture and re-season, if necessary. Spoon on to warm plates, drizzle with olive oil and sprinkle with the remaining parsley before serving with crusty bread.

Halibut is one of my favourite fish. It is meaty, firm and sweet and is perfect for the slow cooker as it is thick enough to cook gently without drying out or falling apart, as it so often does when cooked conventionally. Wrapping it in oak-smoked bacon adds a wonderful richness of flavour and the puy lentils are the perfect base to cook and serve it on.

bacon-wrapped halibut on puy lentils in red wine

SERVES 4

60 ml/4 tbsp olive oil
1 onion, halved and thinly sliced
1 garlic clove, crushed
1 large carrot, diced
1 turnip, diced
2 celery sticks, chopped
350 g/12 oz/2 cups puy lentils
300 ml/½ pt/1¼ cups red wine
900 ml/1½ pts/3¾ cups fish or chicken stock
30 ml/2 tbsp tomato purée (paste)

5 ml/1 tsp unrefined caster (superfine) sugar
Salt and freshly ground black pepper
8 fresh sage leaves, plus extra small ones to garnish
4 pieces of halibut fillet, about 150 g/5 oz each
4 thin rashers (slices) of extra-lean oak-smoked back bacon

TO SERVE:
Crusty bread and a crisp green salad

1 Heat the oil in a frying pan, add the prepared vegetables and fry, stirring, for 2 minutes. Tip into the crock pot and add the lentils.

2 Pour the wine and stock into the frying pan and bring to the boil. Stir in the tomato purée and sugar, then pour over the lentils. Season well, cover and cook on High for 3 hours until the lentils are just tender.

3 Meanwhile, put 2 sage leaves on each piece of fish. Season well with pepper, then wrap each piece in a slice of bacon.

4 When the lentils are cooked, turn down the cooker to Low and put the fish on top of the lentils, with the end flap of bacon underneath. Cover and cook for a further 1 hour until the fish is tender.

5 Carefully lift the fish out of the slow cooker and set aside. Spoon the lentils on to warm plates, lay the fish on top and garnish with a few small sage leaves. Serve with crusty bread and a green salad.

This is simplicity itself but gorgeous all the same! As you will know, fish doesn't take long in the slow cooker, so the cabbage must be very finely shredded to ensure that it cooks in the same time. It's worth noting that whenever a recipe calls for cider, apple juice can be substituted and will give a very similar result – but without the alcohol, of course!

turbot in cidered cabbage with melted cheese

SERVES 4

¼ small green cabbage, very finely shredded

200 ml/7 fl oz/scant 1 cup medium-sweet cider

4 pieces of turbot, about 150 g/5 oz each

2 tomatoes, sliced

100 g/4 oz Cheddar cheese, thinly sliced

Salt and freshly ground black pepper

8 fresh basil leaves

TO SERVE:

Fresh crusty bread

1 Spread out the cabbage in the crock pot.

2 Bring the cider to the boil in a small saucepan and pour over the cabbage. Lay the fish on the cabbage, then top with the tomato slices, followed by the cheese.

3 Season everything lightly with salt and pepper, then cover and cook on Low for 2 hours until the fish is cooked through and the cabbage is tender.

4 Carefully lift off the fish and set aside. Spoon the cabbage and cider into warm open soup plates and top with the fish. Garnish each serving with a couple of basil leaves and serve with crusty bread.

Slow-cooking any type of poultry is guaranteed to keep it moist and succulent. It also saves masses of fuel – you just pop it in a very hot oven for the last 40 minutes to firm up the flesh and to crisp and brown the skin at the same time as you cook the roast potatoes. You are also left with the perfect stock for the most flavoursome gravy you could imagine.

slow-cooked festive bird with fresh cranberry and sausagemeat stuffing

SERVES 6–8

50 g/2 oz fresh cranberries
15 ml/1 tbsp unrefined caster (superfine) sugar
100 g/4 oz pork sausagemeat
50 g/2 oz/1 cup fresh breadcrumbs
30 ml/2 tbsp chopped fresh thyme
30 ml/2 tbsp chopped fresh parsley
Salt and freshly ground black pepper
Sunflower oil for brushing and greasing

1 large oven-ready chicken or a small turkey or turkey crown, about 2.5 kg/5½ lb
600 ml/1 pt/2½ cups boiling chicken or turkey stock
60 ml/4 tbsp plain (all-purpose) flour
90 ml/6 tbsp water

TO SERVE:
Your usual vegetable accompaniments

1   Toss the cranberries in the sugar, then mix with the sausagemeat, breadcrumbs and herbs and season well (I use my hands to work it all together).

2   Use some of this mixture to stuff the neck end of the bird or the crown and secure the flap of skin with a skewer. Put the remaining stuffing on a piece of greased foil and fold up to form a parcel.

3   Place a double thickness of foil in the crock pot so it comes up the sides of the pot (to enable easy removal of the bird after cooking). Brush the foil with oil.

4   Place the bird on the foil in the crock pot. Brush with oil and sprinkle with salt. Rest the foil pack of stuffing on the leg ends if cooking a whole bird or, if cooking a crown, put it at the end where there is most room. Pour the boiling stock around, cover and cook on High for 3–4 hours or Low for 6–8 hours until the bird is cooked through.

5 Using the foil, lift the bird out of the pot and transfer to a roasting tin (still on the foil). Roast in a preheated oven at 220°C/425°F/ gas 7/fan oven 200°C for 40 minutes to brown and crisp. Remove from the oven and leave to rest for 10 minutes before carving.

6 Meanwhile, blend the flour with the water in a saucepan. Blend in the cooking stock, bring to the boil and cook for 2 minutes, stirring. Season to taste, then strain into a gravy boat.

7 Carve the bird and serve with the gravy, stuffing and your usual accompaniments.

For smaller appetites, cut the pheasants into quarters and serve eight people, though you may need to increase the cornflour, stock, brandy and tomato purée slightly to make enough of the delicious sauce to go round. You'll just have to use our own judgement about how much you'll need! Alternatively, halve the quantities and cook in a small slow cooker.

brace of pheasant with bacon, beetroot and apples

SERVES 4

75 ml/5 tbsp cornflour (cornstarch)
Salt and freshly ground black pepper
1 brace of pheasant, halved
25 g/1 oz/2 tbsp butter
4 cooked baby beetroot (red beets), quartered
100 g/4 oz button mushrooms, sliced
2 Cox's apples, quartered, cored and fairly thickly sliced
4 rashers (slices) of smoked streaky bacon, rinded and diced

12–16 whole shallots, peeled
2 celery sticks, finely chopped
250 ml/8 fl oz/1 cup chicken stock
30 ml/2 tbsp brandy
15 ml/1 tbsp balsamic vinegar
15 ml/1 tbsp tomato purée (paste)
2.5 ml/½ tsp dried mixed herbs
Chopped fresh parsley to garnish

TO SERVE:
Fluffy mashed potatoes and a green salad

1   Season the cornflour with a little salt and pepper and use to coat the pheasant pieces.

2   Heat half the butter in a frying pan, add the pheasant and brown all over. Transfer to the crock pot. Scatter the beetroot and mushroom and apple slices around.

3   Heat the remaining butter in the frying pan, add the bacon, shallots and celery and cook, stirring for 2 minutes. Blend the stock into any remaining cornflour, then stir into the pan with the brandy, balsamic vinegar and tomato purée. Bring to the boil and season to taste.

4   Pour over the pheasant and sprinkle with the mixed herbs. Cover and cook on High for 3–4 hours or Low for 6–8 hours (depending on how tender the pheasant is).

5   Taste and re-season, if necessary. Sprinkle with a little parsley and serve with fluffy mashed potatoes and a green salad.

You can make this in advance and store it in the fridge in a clean screw-topped jar or other sealed container until you need it. It is, of course, perfect with your Christmas turkey but is equally delicious with gammon, pork, chicken or cheeses – particularly goat's or soft ripe ones like Brie or Camembert. If you prefer, use orange juice instead of wine.

cranberry sauce
with red wine

SERVES ABOUT 8

350 g/12 oz fresh cranberries
175 g/6 oz/¾ cup unrefined caster
  (superfine) sugar

150 ml/¼ pt/⅔ cup red wine

1 Put the cranberries in a small crock pot or in a dish that will fit in a large one. Pour in enough boiling water to come half-way up the sides of the pot or bowl. Add the sugar.

2 Bring the wine to the boil in a small saucepan and pour over. Cover and cook on High for 2 hours until the fruit 'pops'.

3 Spoon into a serving dish and leave to cool before serving.

This Christmas pudding turns out rich, dark and delicious in the slow cooker and you'll only need to top up the boiling water once or twice – much easier than conventional steaming or boiling. I use more breadcrumbs and less flour than most recipes to give a lovely light result. Don't forget to let all the family have a stir and make a wish at step 2!

christmas pudding
with apple brandy and walnuts

MAKES 1 LARGE PUDDING

500 g/18 oz/3 cups dried mixed fruit (fruit cake mix)

75 g/3 oz/¾ cup shelled walnuts, chopped

45 ml/3 tbsp apple brandy or cognac

2 unpeeled Cox's or other red and yellow skinned sweet apples, grated

100 g/4 oz/1 cup shredded suet

75 g/3 oz/⅓ cup unrefined dark brown sugar

175 g/6 oz/3 cups fresh wholemeal breadcrumbs

1 large egg, beaten

50 g/2 oz/½ cup plain (all-purpose) flour

5 ml/1 tsp mixed (apple pie) spice

1.5 ml/¼ tsp grated nutmeg

1.5 ml/¼ tsp ground cinnamon

150 ml/¼ pt/⅔ cup Guinness or brown beer

1 Mix the fruit and nuts with the apple brandy or cognac and leave to soak for 2–3 hours.

2 Thoroughly mix in all the remaining ingredients.

3 Grease a 1.2 litre/2 pt/5 cup pudding basin and line the base with a round of non-stick baking parchment. Spoon the pudding into the basin and press down well. Cover with a round of non-stick baking parchment, then a saucer that fits neatly on top. Cover the basin with a double thickness of foil, twisting and folding under the rim to secure.

4 Stand the basin in the crock pot and pour round enough boiling water to come at least half-way up the side of the basin. Cover and cook on High for 10–13 hours, topping up with boiling water as necessary, until the pudding is as dark as you like.

5 Leave to cool, then re-wrap in clean foil and store in a cool, dark place. On Christmas day, cook again in its wrappings on High for 4–5 hours.

INDEX